Mentoring
Intentional
Excellence

A Guide for Early- and Mid-Career Professionals

J. Wayne Stewart

SGR Publishing
Allen, Texas

Mentoring Intentional Excellence
A Guide for Early- and Mid-Career Professionals

SGR Publishing
Allen, Texas

Book Design: Robin Simonds, Beagle Bay, Inc.

ISBN: 978-0-9974450-1-5
LCCN: 2017905521

First Edition
Printed in the United States of America
22 21 20 19 18 17   1 2 3 4 5 6 7 8 9 10

Acknowledgments

This book is dedicated to my teachers and mentors over many years; the people who invested their wisdom and time in me. Some of them didn't know they were teaching me at the time, but I hope I was able to incorporate in my management style the best of them.

I want to thank those who spent time reviewing the drafts and making suggestions for improvement. Specifically, my wife, Dottie and my son, Brad, who know me best and to whom I gave permission to be honest. Also, thank you to business associates and friends, Shon Anderson, Jeff Smith, and Tom and Laura Longmire, who I value greatly for our shared values and professionalism. They were not shy about sharing their suggestions and knowledge of world-class business practices.

Finally, I want to thank Jacqueline Simonds who first conceived of the potential for this book, while she was helping me prepare and publish my first book.

To all of you, and to those who read my thoughts on lifelong learning and its effect on my forty-five year career, I say thank you.

Contents

Foreword

Every up-and-coming leader needs mentors. The farther you want to go, the more you'll need them. Nobody gets far on their own. Once in the executive ranks, success depends on your ability to learn. Almost everyone is smart and hard-working. Those are just tickets to the game, not enough to win.

Trouble is, finding a senior executive to mentor you and then actually finding time on both your calendars to spend enough hours together to absorb a career full of their learning can take years of lunches.

You're blessed to be holding *Mentoring Intentional Excellence*, a career's worth of stories, lessons, and tough questions from a senior executive with a proven track record of results, guided by a foundation of values that will keep you on solid footing and guide you in calm or stormy seas. I've been blessed to be mentored by Wayne Stewart in and outside the corporate environment for a number of years. I confess that I'm not sure I was smart enough to choose him as a mentor. I think he chose me.

One of the qualities I appreciated most about Wayne is his desire to see me be the best that I can be. His push and questioning challenged me many times, made me uncomfortable a few times, but always came with my best interest at heart. I believe that to be a differentiator of a truly great mentor.

Wayne helped me through some highs, lows, and major challenges by sharing his own experience and perspective through the lens of his core values: integrity, commitment to excellence, and having fun.

That last one caught you off guard, didn't it? Leading people and/or businesses is serious business, pardon the pun. To survive the pressure, you've got to surround yourself with great people and have some fun along the way. Wayne set a great example of how to lead well, execute well, and keep it fun.

If you're looking for a mentor you can trust and allow to shape your view of the business world, expand your view of your role as a manager and executive, and challenge you with admissions of pitfalls so you can avoid them, this is your mentoring relationship. I'm excited for you to turn the pages and get into *Mentoring Intentional Excellence*. I believe that Wayne's honesty and wisdom learned through experience will be an asset to you as it is to me.

Lucky for you, it won't take years to get all the conversations in! Enjoy,

Shon Anderson, CEO
B9Creations

Mentoring
Intentional
Excellence

Chapter One
How to Use This Book

This book is arranged in two parts. In Part One, imagine that we've met—either professionally or through some personal acquaintance—and you decide that you'd like advice on some aspects of your professional life. We go to a coffee shop and sit down for a cup and a talk. Like anyone in their early- to mid-career, you probably have a lot of questions. (Even after a lifetime working with corporations and as an entrepreneur, I assure you, I do too.) I offer to mentor you if you are interested.

You then tell me about your work and pose some questions. I listen carefully, then we talk. Sometimes I give you direct suggestions, but other times, instead of a direct answer, I tell you a story of my own, drawn from almost fifty years of experience. Some of the stories are funny. Some are deadly serious. And some are heart-breaking. All of them illuminate something. I often tell you what I am driving at. But you probably won't remember that part. You will probably remember the story. That's how humans are. We recall meaningful narratives, rather than direct "advice."

It would be wonderful to sit down with each person who has this book and talk to you personally (and yes, I'm willing do that if you'd like. See the last chapter). But this is a book of "Infonuggets" (a term originated by publishing consultant Jacqueline Simonds to describe today's age of rapid-fire information-consumption) and not a conversation. You are likely a busy person and want answers right away. I've arranged this book in topics that might apply to your work life. Subjects such as "Dancing with Your People," "Battling The Octopus," and "Finishing Well Intentionally" contain experiences that relate directly to situations and challenges you might find yourself dealing with. While not chronologically arranged, I've tried to include context that will help you understand the career phase in which I found myself at the time. You are welcome to skip around the chapters (although I hope you'll take the time to read all of it). Many of the stories may help you, even if you don't know you're looking for advice in a particular area.

In Part Two, we're not at a coffee shop. This time, we're in a conference and I'll be presenting the ideas behind the stories in Part I. Rather than providing experiences in this section, I've extracted career advice for dealing with things as diverse as "Managing Your Boss" to "The Stewart Theory of Change Management," and "The Management Punch List."

A brief summary of my professional career begins with Texas Instruments in 1973, lasting twenty-one years as I moved up the management chain to lead global operations and businesses. From 1994, I began my executive career, serving as Vice President, Executive Vice President, Board Member, and Chairman for several companies. After 2001, I went out on my own, founding four businesses and serving on several Boards, both corporate and charitable. At the request of an old friend, I returned to the corporate world for the last few years of my career, finally retiring for good in 2013. In all that time and in all those roles I was constantly reminded that I didn't have all the answers. Consulting the knowledge of others always improved my decisions and made me a better manager.

I hope you find this book of use to you in your work-life journey!

Part One: The Stories

Every new start should be purposeful, with intentional learning,
changing, and succeeding.

Chapter Two

Intentional Beginnings

How you begin and how you finish are the bookends for important transitions in your career. They define you in first- and last-impressions. Your character is recognized by others as they see how you work. Remember, others are always watching, and they measure you by the way you handle successes … and failures. So here's a series of "beginnings" from my career, along with the lessons learned and purposeful changes that helped define my career.

Mayflower Moving Company

As have so many before me, my work life started with summer jobs. Undoubtedly the worst I had was working for Mayflower Moving Company. I arrived every morning at 7:00 a.m. at the Mayflower Warehouse, one of ten high school kids who were grunt labor. Mayflower truck drivers drove into town with loads to deliver or pick up, and they came by the warehouse to pick up "grunts" for a day. Some of the drivers were good guys, working alongside us, giving directions and operating as a team, but others dropped the trailer and headed for a bar, leaving us to load/ unload the truck. We hauled boxes, furniture, and appliances in or out of houses non-stop for the entire day. It was hot, back-breaking work, and although I was in good condition, it was exhausting, mindless work. Mayflower management had few standards for packing and loading operations, and they put little oversight into what happened "in the field."

This was a major weakness and an early lesson on the need for field supervision (quality control). It's critical when you're dealing with customers and employees. When accidents and/or injuries occur, you must be able to demonstrate

> All honest jobs and the people who do them are worthy of respect.

you have appropriate standards, policies, procedures, and oversight in place to protect customers and employees.

That Mayflower gig was a terrible job, and as soon as I got another offer, I was outta there.

Prestonwood Country Club

The summer after my college freshman year, I worked at Prestonwood Country Club where I helped build the golf course. It was a good job working outdoors, learning leadership skills, and getting a great tan. My wisdom teeth had been extracted the day before I started work at the golf course, and my jaws were bleeding and killing me. I spat blood for two weeks until the pits healed, so I was not in good shape for an outdoor job of hard labor. But I was determined to work there, so I didn't tell anyone.

On the first day, the boss told us we would have a job for two weeks in order to get over the initial hump, then the group would be cut back to six workers for the rest of the summer. I was determined to be one of the workers kept on, so I took on every assignment and worked hard to satisfy the boss. He took a liking to me and gave me assignments that tested my abilities. In those first two weeks, we mowed fairways and greens, removed and cut up trees, laid turf, and dug and filled sand traps. I took on every assignment enthusiastically, and the boss was watching. At the end of two weeks, I was one of the workers kept on, and I was put in charge of two others. Our team of three did more work in half a day than the other team did all day long.

I met the architect, pro-golfer Don January, on several occasions when he walked the course and made design changes. He brought his clubs to the course and one of us caddied for him as he hit shots from all over the course. He'd call us over and direct us to make changes in fairways, greens, traps, tree lines, etc. It was up to us to

> The rewards of hard work can often be as simple as keeping your job. Most often they're so much more.

mark the changes and implement them before his next visit. He was a nice enough fellow, although a bit demanding and aloof.

The Prestonwood job was great for a kid who loved golf, lasting through the summer until I returned to the University of Texas. I learned the value of hard work, competing with other employees, supervising others, and dealing with executives.

Delta Steel Buildings

On the unpleasant side of the ledger, the next summer I worked as a "torch man" at Delta Steel Buildings, and it was brutal. We worked in an un-air conditioned, sheet metal building with a sand floor over concrete. The building was full of torch men and welders working on steel building structures that were shipped to the field for assembly. By 8:00 a.m., the temperature was over 100 degrees in the building, and by the end of the day it was even hotter.

At lunchtime, I normally slumped on the floor and rested while eating a sandwich. However, many employees went immediately to a work table and shot craps for thirty minutes. What I saw was unbelievable. Some of the men had gambling problems, betting every bit of cash they had on them—sometimes even their jewelry and paychecks. I saw one fellow get mad one day and go to his car for its title, which he proceeded to lose. These were blue collar workers with families, and they could lose two weeks of food money in fifteen minutes, then beg for credit so they could lose more.

Management has the responsibility for monitoring working conditions and making environmental changes that enable employees to be productive and focused on the quality of the work product. Likewise, employee behavior on company premises should be a management concern, and when it negatively affects performance, it needs to be eliminated. When the dust clears, gambling often results in regrets and hard feelings, and it shouldn't be tolerated.

The work day finished at 3:00 p.m., and I was exhausted, typically losing eight-to-ten pounds daily. I headed straight home, showered, and tried to replenish. Some nights, I had a date, but I wasn't very good company. At the end of the summer, I swore off manual labor and went to summer school the next two years.

Summer and interim jobs were hugely instructive for a newbie entering the work force. Viewing the world from the bottom taught me volumes about successful employee work conditions. As a supervisor and manager, you should always keep communication lines open with employees at all levels of the organization. Take time to go to

> I learned from these manual labor jobs that I wanted to earn my living with my head, and not my back.

operational areas and sit down with the people who touch the products and customers. After all, that's where the rubber meets the road, and they will often have different views of the world, sometimes so different that you absolutely must be willing to hear and deal with them.

Professional Launch

In the fall of 1972, my last semester at the University of Texas, I applied to a number of companies through the UT Placement Office. I was one of hundreds interviewing with the same group of bored Human Resources people in tiny, stuffy cubicles. I felt like I was a piece of meat being run through a processing plant. Though a couple of interviews resulted in follow-ups, none resulted in a job offer.

INTENTIONAL BEGINNINGS

In December 1972, I packed up my UT dorm room for the last time, said goodbye to Austin, and drove home to Dallas with a huge sense of relief. After the Christmas holidays, I began networking and visiting local companies to fill out applications. There was no internet back then, so everything was done on foot and in person.

> Relationships get you the job, so be authentic and try to establish personal connections.

I walked in the door at the Texas Instruments Employment Office in late January 1973, filled out an application, and went on my way. A week later, I got a call to come in for interviews, where I talked to six people. The only one I remember was the warehouse manager, Dennis Smith—he and I hit it off immediately. We spent part of the interview talking about hunting, guns, and other fun stuff, and I guess I did well enough in the interviews to get a job offer. I started work at TI's Richardson, Texas site on February 26, 1973, beginning a twenty-one-year stint at TI.

Today, there are numerous websites with advice on how to manage your job search, but don't assume you'll find a good job on a job board.

The Newbie

Texas Instruments was an incredible training ground for a kid straight out of college, and I was fortunate to get a job that tossed me immediately into the fire. That's a fundamental difference between us Baby Boomers and subsequent generations. Back then, formal training programs were few and far between, and work skills came via hard knocks and on-the-job training. In the ensuing years, companies have become more willing to invest in employees with orientation programs, training classes, rotational programs, and other support. Better or not, today there's a lot more attention paid to on-boarding employees, with fewer expectations for delivering immediate results early in their careers.

Day One, I was put in charge of eight employees, all of whom had years of experience at TI. I learned early-on that I had better listen before opening my mouth, ask for suggestions before making decisions, and have my facts straight when it was time to disagree. I learned an important lesson from my first boss, Ben Teel, who had been with TI for thirty years. He encouraged me to aggressively take charge and make things happen. I had to take personal risks and be willing to be held accountable.

As great a training ground as TI was, it was definitely old-school when it came to the work environment. Although ethics and integrity were clearly defined and upheld, the culture was largely "take no prisoners," and the weak did not survive long. It became clear that I had to make some changes. Except for sports, I had been a "follower" through the first twenty-two years of my life, and I was short on self-confidence. I realized that an unassertive personality wasn't going to survive at TI. I had a talk with myself, convinced that I had to change my personality to become more assertive and develop leadership skills in order to compete at TI. It never occurred to me that TI was a bad place to work; it was up to me to adapt to the requirements and environment. Over time, when I was right more times than wrong, I learned to push with diplomacy, and others not only accepted my leadership, they welcomed it.

> People want a leader who is confident and willing to take responsibility.

I watched others, identifying strengths and weaknesses, and recognizing motivations. Seeing both positive and negative traits in others, I made conscious decisions about my management style, adopting those that were positive and effective, and excluding those I felt were negative, damaging, or de-motivating. I became a good observer of others, a skill

> Embrace intentional change. Don't wait for someone to give you authority; you must take it and exercise it appropriately.

that served me well my whole career. Life is a never-ending opportunity to learn and improve, and my management style did a lot of adapting over the years, as I found people I wanted to emulate … or not.

The First Job . . . and My First Intentional Change

My first professional job was Production Control Supervisor in Texas Instruments $1+ billion Defense Business (the Equipment Group). It was spread across multiple sites, producing defense equipment with technologies ranging from radar and electro-optics, to missile and bomb guidance, to satellite systems.

Paveway was the name of a family of products that utilized Laser Guided Bomb (LGB) technology. It was an innovative, low-cost weapon that provided in-flight guidance for a family of smart bombs launched from airplanes. While they didn't fly or glide, these free-fall bombs were extremely accurate when guided to ground targets; they were revolutionary for the time. TI supplied thousands of first-generation (Paveway I) smart bombs to the U.S. Air Force and Navy during the Viet Nam War. The large production contracts had just completed, and production was scaling back to 400 systems per month as a second generation system (Paveway II) was in development.

As Production Control Supervisor for Paveway programs, most of my work took place on the assembly line. We assembled electronics, control, and guidance systems in a high-security environment. My job was to schedule and maintain the status of production operations, moving parts from the warehouse to the manufacturing lines, and completed systems to the shipping department. Though the 120 assembly workers on two shifts didn't report to me, I was responsible for scheduling their work and supplying them with materials and supplies to ensure maximum productivity. I chaired weekly production meetings and managed the computer systems for the entire production program.

Early on, I decided I needed to understand how the Paveway system was built and operated, and I asked a lot of questions about operational parameters and performance. Some of my questions were probably mundane, but here's my take on "stupid questions." First, they are often not stupid, and when asked with an air of interest and willingness to learn, most people are patient. Asking "dumb" questions is not only acceptable, but desirable when done in a positive way and with the intention to learn.

> I was willing to learn from others—I *wanted* to learn from them.

In the end, my natural inquisitiveness paid off when I was recognized for leadership, and I soon learned more than my peers about the products. This served me well when the boss was looking for someone to conduct a tour or orient a new employee. Both are ways to gain credibility.

Being the Good Soldier, Even When It Doesn't Fit

Fast-forward through sixteen years of successes, multiple promotions, and experience managing large Defense operations. I was asked to take over a newly-formed division in Texas Instrument's Information Technology Group (ITG). The day I walked in the door, my new position with the 500-person global Enterprise Systems Business (ESB) was a challenge. The main problem was the culture of this division.

For any internal support organization, the operating business units are The Customers. Providing responsive support and achieving customer satisfaction should be the primary criteria for the support organization's success. Unfortunately, TI's IT organization was so technically focused that it determined its own measures of success—generally having little to do with customer satisfaction or support.

After years of unresolved complaints, TI's executive committee decided to try an experiment to redefine the culture of the IT organization to become more customer-centric. I was the experiment, and it was up to me to change the attitude and culture of the organization, a mandate that wasn't popular with the organization, the CIO (my new boss), nor the President of ITG (my boss's boss). When I addressed the issue of customer-centricity, the people in my organization gave me a blank look and a standard answer, "We don't have enough budget to be customer-responsive." Yet they always had enough budget to explore new technolo-

> For a new assignment, be sure you recognize the warts and have strong executive support to do what's necessary, including sacrificing some sacred cows.

gies. In other words, "Send us more money, and we'll pay more attention to our customers." This came at a time of mandate to cut IT costs by almost fifty percent over three years.

When you're trying to change the culture of an entrenched organization, you must have strong executive support and dogged determination. Even then, it sometimes requires you to make an example of high-profile employees who don't support your vision. If they fail to deliver their support, take action in a way that clearly demonstrates you're in charge and willing to make hard decisions.

Despite what I was promised when I walked in the door, my bosses didn't really care about changing. When things didn't go well, I was singled out for blame. As two of my executive peers in the Defense business told me later, I was doomed to failure from the beginning. This assignment was my first career failure.

FSI International

Fast forward again a few years to a time after leaving Texas Instruments and joining FSI International in 1994, I began an exciting new job as V.P. of Operations. After the first twenty-one years of my career in a huge corporation, moving to FSI was a dramatic change. It was a small public company on the verge of major growth in a dynamic industry, expanding its customer base with diverse product lines. The company had

finished its prior year at $88 million of sales and good profitability, but its facilities, IT systems, and manufacturing capabilities were stretched badly. The growth plan projected doubling in size in less than two years, and it demanded a new model.

> Don't be tentative when addressing the challenges of a new assignment.

I commuted between Dallas and Minneapolis for six months until we relocated to Eden Prairie, a suburb of Minneapolis close to FSI's headquarters in Chaska. I had to make early decisions supporting FSI's growth plans and taking cost out of the company's operations. As V.P. of Operations (later Executive V.P. of Global Operations), I was responsible for Manufacturing, Materials, Facilities, and IT. My incumbent managers had grown up with the business, but they had no experience managing a rapidly-expanding company. Some were holding the company back, so I opened executive searches for Manufacturing, IT, and Purchasing Managers. Three long-time Texas Instruments' friends soon joined me at FSI. Tom Longmire became FSI's Director of Purchasing, Ken Weis became IT Infrastructure Systems Manager, and Joanie Weis came to FSI in a senior administrative role. A new CIO and Manufacturing Manager were hired, and we were successful at retaining the prior managers and their experience. Everyone supported our shared vision, and FSI's executives and the Board were strong allies.

Having learned from my TI IT assignment, I performed a ninety-day assessment, identifying challenges realistically, along with an action plan. I presented the assessment to the executive staff, gaining input and support. While leadership changes were difficult, handled with honesty and open communications, we were able to retain the prior managers and their support.

Director Experience

In 1996, FSI International acquired a company in southern England, and since it was an English subsidiary, we were required to form a separate Board of Directors to operate under British law. By then, I was E.V.P. of Global Operations and felt I could gain international experience by sitting on the governing board of the acquired company. I suggested the idea to my boss, CEO Joel Elftmann, and he agreed. I spent

> Learning about foreign cultures is mandatory to successfully compete. The global marketplace puts a premium on managers who have international experience.

the next two years working periodically overseas. The trips to the southern coast of England were enjoyable, and I became good friends with the President of the U.K. company. The whole experience was worthwhile, even with the terrible logistics of overseas travel at the back of the plane.

Telecom, Here I Come

After the semiconductor equipment industry took a severe nosedive in 1998 and FSI International was forced to reorganize, once again I launched my search for a senior executive position. My wife, Dottie, and I decided we wanted to move back to Texas to be close to our families, but we needed our next company to pay for the move. So, I targeted Dallas-based companies and operations for my job search. As a senior executive, I knew my highest probability of success would come through networking. We made a trip to Dallas, where I organized meetings with executives in the area. That's where I met Lonnie Martin, Senior V.P. with ADC Telecommunications. ADC was a $3 billion telecommunications equipment company with (coincidentally) headquarters in Minnesota, a short distance from our home in Eden Prairie. Lonnie and I hit it off immediately, and he pointed me to Bill Cadogan, President, CEO, and Chairman of the company. I returned to Minneapolis and met with Bill for a get-acquainted visit, which went well, and I was brought back for an entire day of interviews with the executive staff.

By now, interviewing for executive positions was easier for me, and I had learned to be myself—more relaxed, engaged, and professional, with an executive's demeanor and vocabulary. I went into each interview looking for common interests and getting comfortable with the new relationship before trying to buy or sell anything. I always learned as much or more in each interview as the person across the table. I collected verbal and visual clues about the person's hot buttons, priorities, and concerns, and patterned my questions and answers to respond to them. Every interview was an opportunity to get to know the individual across the table, much as I had when I first talked with Lonnie.

Conversations with the executive team went well, and I learned that the company had the challenge faced by many high-growth, acquisitive companies—integrating the company to achieve synergies and drive cost out of the combined company. The executive who led the largest and fastest-growing division in the company had already established disciplined operations and wanted no outside interference. My approach with him was to go after "corporate overhead" problems. Another executive had a struggling electronics business, with operations scattered all over the company due to a series of poorly-integrated acquisition. My approach with him was to suggest ways to streamline and add discipline to his internal operations. Other executives were managing operations that were inefficient and "below critical mass," so my approach with them was to leverage cross-divisional operations. The CEO and CFO wanted to know how I would attack corporate inefficiencies (the CFO called it "corporate bloat") and improve profitability. Intentionally listening first, I was able to pattern my responses to the specific needs of each of the individuals I visited with. It didn't hurt that the V.P. of Human Resources, Laura Owen, had been Human Resources Manager at one of my Texas Instruments' plants a decade earlier. Amazing how things go 'round, isn't it? The two of us had a lot of catching up to do, and she was in my corner from the beginning.

After interviews and negotiations, I was offered the job of V.P. of Corporate Operations, a newly created position to streamline the operations of the company. In 1998, I started work at ADC before my FSI severance ran out, and coupled with my office being fifteen minutes from our home, the change of positions worked out perfectly. I also negotiated a company-paid relocation back home to Texas, so I was off and running with my third company.

> At the executive level, networking is the best job search avenue.

I made a whirlwind listening tour, and began putting together a strategy of corporate consolidation to drive cost out of the company. While the executive staff agreed with the objective, it was a role that was viewed with suspicion. One executive even viewed me as a threat. More on that subject a little later.

As a senior manager/executive in search of your next opportunity, spend most of your time networking. Answering ads and following Internet job boards have a much lower probability of success. Instead, leverage prior relationships, asking for meetings to "pick their brains" for help with your search. These meetings always result in relationship-building, and you'd be surprised how many times something you say or hear will trigger discussion about challenges the other person needs help with. You're always interviewing, whether formally or casually, and you never know when it may lead to your next position. When the interviews go well, a position may be created just for you.

Chairman of TAC Critical Systems

Let's jump forward several years to 2007. While shutting down Mega Wraps—my exploration of my entrepreneurial side—I re-opened Stewart Consulting and reconnected with one of my Texas Instruments work buddies, Dean Meyer, President of TAC Americas. TAC was a Sweden-based building automation company, subsequently bought by the French company, Schneider Electric (SE). Dean called one day to invite me to be a director of a subsidiary being formed in Washington, D.C. Since TAC was foreign-owned, an Ameri-can-chartered corporation was required to perform classified work for the government. I joined the board of TAC's new venture, TAC Critical Systems, Inc., where I re-activated my security clearances so I could be-gin working with the company quickly.

> Always be available for unexpected opportunities that seemingly come out of nowhere.

When the Board first met, it was obvious the company needed leadership for organizing and planning the new entity, especially when working with the Federal Government. I was elected Chairman and as-sisted the company in developing an organizational structure, processes, procedures, and systems. As Chairman, I supported and represented the company, developing leadership processes for the new company, and ne-gotiating procedures between the company and the government. This was a very profitable time for Stewart Consulting Company.

Back to the Corporate World for the Last Time

After eighteen months as Chairman of TAC Critical Systems, I got another call from Dean. This time, he asked me to come to work for him directly at Schneider Electric, and it presented a quandary. I wasn't keen about going back to work in a large corporation, but Dean outlined some specific issues he needed help with, including working with him directly as an advisor. In early 2007, I accepted Dean's offer to join TAC as V.P. of Mergers & Acquisitions and Customer Quality. I told my wife, Dottie, it would last three years, and I sincerely meant it, but with all the economic turmoil of 2008–2010, I ultimately stayed for six years.

Intentional Beginnings

SE was an $18 billion global company which had been on an acqui-sition binge for a decade, and Dean asked me to do three things: create a successful customer satisfaction program, assist with acquisitions, and mentor him as the president of the company. I had no further upward career aspirations, and I was given the freedom to define my job and work on strategies

> The best situation you can have is one in which you are able to work fearlessly and boldly manage your organization.

that challenged and supported the business. I really enjoyed the freedom of being the senior advisor in a dynamic company, able to speak the truth as I saw it, go where there was the most bang for the buck, and make decisions without worrying about the fall-out. This was the most enjoy-able and rewarding time of my career, although I chafed under the heavy yoke of SE's bureaucracy.

During my time at SE, my responsibilities expanded at the request of my customers, to take over purchasing, customer training and sup-port, and marketing support. We built a high-performance team whose number one priority was customer support, focusing on customers and customer-facing organizations with speed and accuracy. We implement-ed initiatives that saved money and served them directly, and they ap-preciated our support to the extent that they offered up some of their budgets so we could add support personnel.

All support organizations live and die on their credibility. It's hard to earn and easy to lose, and those that have it are viewed as hav-ing integrity and a passion for supporting others. We always treated our customers (external and internal) proactively, with the objective of fulfilling every commitment on-schedule *and*

> Support organizations live and die based on their credibility, hard to earn and easy to lose.

under-budget. Responsiveness, competency, value-added initiatives, and transparency all contributed to our credibility, and by the time I left the company, my team numbered more than thirty customer support personnel.

Wait . . . Was that a Job Interview?

During my time with Schneider Electric, our work was interrupted on numerous occasions by the S.E.'s French HQ as it launched initiatives and bureaucracies to "help" us be more successful. If you suspect you're detecting some cynicism on my part related to corporate bureaucracies, you would be correct. See the chapter, "Battling the Octopus."

When SE launched an initiative to form a universal Quality organization (it opened its doors with more than thirty senior managers), we were forced to respond by forming a global TAC Global Quality Network (GQN) to respond to HQ. I took over leadership of the global network, without adding any headcount, and we went to work aligning processes and reporting systems *without adding headcount*. We supported TAC's Executive Committee (ExCom) with quality data, while responding to SE edicts. A year later, I was attending an ExCom meeting, when TAC's global president unexpectedly announced he was leaving, and a new president would be taking over. The new president (I'll call him Bill) was present, and he assumed the helm that day. Since I was there, I took the opportunity to meet with him to get a reading on his priorities. We talked for thirty minutes, and I thought we had a good dialog.

Bill had come from an enormous U. S. electrical products business, where he had risen quickly up the management and executive ranks. He was a big-company guy, who set about immediately putting infrastructure in place that the prior president would never have allowed. We started looking more like a big-company, bureaucratically-controlled organization, rather than the responsive, customer-focused, lean-and-mean management structure under prior leadership. Bill immediately identified the need for a Global S.V.P. of Quality and Process Excellence, and I sent him an email suggesting that I wanted to be considered for the position. I was leading the GQN and was a natural candidate for the new global S.V.P. role. But I suspect Bill viewed me as too old (I was sixty), too decentralized, and too dogmatic in working for business independence. I didn't even get the courtesy of an interview or phone call before I was told I was not in consideration.

Ultimately, I'm glad I didn't get the job. The new role wasn't a good fit for me, since I would have been badly frustrated by corporate interference and loss of business autonomy. I watched the manager who did get the job, Jeff Wood, travel the world, con-

> Be careful what you wish for, and don't let your ego push you into a decision you'll come to regret.

tinually jerked around, and often hung out to dry by the SE bureaucracy.

After a few months, I was officially transferred under Jeff as V.P. of Process Excellence & Quality for SE's Buildings Business in the Americas. It took a few months, but it worked out well. Jeff became a strong supporter and great boss. He acknowledged my help in learning the business and mentoring him in his new role.

Chapter Three

Safety First

I never had the horrible experience of seeing one of my employees badly injured or killed while on the job. But I saw enough serious accidents elsewhere to establish some very important priorities in my management process. Right alongside ethics and integrity, the safety and

> Never take the safety and well-being of your employees for granted.

well-being of your employees must be at the top of the list. Before it was popular with my peers, early in my career I made the decision that I would never be the cause of one of my people being injured, and I intentionally adopted closed-loop processes for formal investigations and corrective actions. You can't afford the repercussions of a major safety failure, and executives who knowingly ignore hazards can be personally prosecuted in the event of a major incident.

Bottling Dr. Pepper

The summer after my junior year in high school, I worked at the historic Dr. Pepper bottling plant on Mockingbird Lane in Dallas. It was not a great job, working as a gopher in the un-air conditioned bottling plant where the stickiest, sweetest products on the face of the Earth were bottled.

This was where I witnessed one of the most dangerous accidents of my career. And I learned what safety means, along with the implications of inadequate response to safety problems. In the bottling plant, filled bottles exiting the bottling line went to the casing station, where twenty-four bottles at a time dropped into wooden cases. The cases were stacked onto wooden pallets *without sides*, six layers of six cases each. The pallets of cased bottles were six-feet tall and semi-stable as they were lifted by forklifts and moved to a storage wall. The entire day's production was positioned against the wall, waiting to be loaded onto delivery trucks early the next morning. The pallets of drinks were stacked three-high, and the top cases were eighteen feet in the air. I admired their skill as the forklift drivers used their gas-operated lift trucks to hoist loads of bottles overhead, while traveling across the plant, and place the pallets one on top of the other, no more than two inches apart.

One fateful day, I watched a forklift driver approach the wall with a pallet load, raising it as he neared the wall, which already had several thousand cases of Dr. Pepper stacked against it. Suddenly, the forklift hit a puddle of Dr. Pepper and slid sideways into the eighteen-foot stack of cases. What happened then was in slow motion, as the stacks began slowly tipping, creating a domino effect. Over the course of fifteen seconds, more than 50,000 bottles hit the floor, breaking and spewing fizzy Dr. Pepper fountains into the air, depositing their twelve ounces of brown liquid sugar into a three-inch deep, ever-expanding pool. The noise was incredible! I can't imagine what it was like for the forklift driver; even with protective bars above his head, he was buried under a huge pile of broken glass, cases, and Dr. Pepper. When we pulled him from under the pile of carnage, he was cursing a blue streak at high volume.

The shift supervisor and general manager were on the floor in minutes, wading with the rest of us into the pool of Dr. Pepper. They hurled orders, and I was appointed to the broom detail, sweeping broken glass, bottles, and wooden cases into piles of debris, and hundreds of gallons of Dr. Pepper into floor drains. Unbroken bottles were salvaged, washed, and re-loaded into cases. Everything was hosed down, and the broken glass and cases were shoveled into barrels and hauled away. It took hours to clean up the mess, and everyone was put on overtime for emergency-bottling to recover lost production in time for morning deliveries. The plant stank of sour Dr. Pepper for weeks, despite numerous hose-downs.

One of the most spectacular failures I've witnessed, we were fortunate no one was seriously injured. We recovered the production plan within a couple of days, but I was amazed that nothing changed on the plant floor. No new safety rules were implemented, and within a week, the forklift drivers and production plant were back to business as usual.

> Every safety failure must be evaluated for root causes, and corrective actions must be implemented immediately.

The only good side of the summer at Dr. Pepper was that I was allowed to drink all the Dr. Pepper products I could handle on a daily basis. After a summer of unlimited Dr. Pepper, it's not my favorite soft drink.

The Western Company

Another summer job was at The Western Company (TWC), an oil field service company. I'd applied in the spring but didn't receive an offer until I'd already begun work at the Mayflower Moving Company (see Chapter 3). When I was offered the TWC job, I gladly quit Mayflower and went to work in TWC's research center. It was here that I gained my introduction to a machine shop and some very interesting projects. It was a terrific job, learning metalworking skills, reading engineering drawings, building prototypes, and learning from senior machinists. It was a friendly work environment, and I would have gladly gone back the next summer if TWC had been hiring.

It was there that I learned about rocket engines via a potentially disastrous accident. A gas cylinder, containing compressed gas, fell off a truck directly onto its valve—which snapped off. The cylinder took off like a rocket, punching through the warehouse wall and destroying equipment inside. It finally "ran out of gas" with no one injured, but lots of damage.

The Western Company was serious about safety, and I witnessed the proper way to evaluate accidents and respond to safety issues, even in a research facility. As you'll read later, research facilities are notorious for bending or disregarding safety policies, and the management chain is ultimately responsible for establishing and holding employees accountable to policies and procedures. The TWC safety investigation revealed that the cylinder's safety cap was missing when it was being unloaded from the truck. Although no one took responsibility for the missing cap, we were trained on how to handle high-pressure gas cylinders and ensure safety caps were not removed until the cylinder was properly restrained.

> Compromised workplace safety is not acceptable. A formal accident investigation and corrective action process is mandatory.

I worked for the rest of the summer at TWC, working on various projects and learning machining and tool shop skills. It was a great summer job.

The Original "MythBusters"

What I learned at that high school job, I applied at Texas Instruments nearly twenty years later. In the early 1980s, we began designing the Paveway III missile manufacturing facility, while still in production of both Paveway I and II systems. The Paveway III design utilized a high-pressure helium canister in the control section to guide the weapon in flight. "The bottle" was the size of a softball, made of high-strength steel, and pressurized with 8,000 pounds per square inch of helium. Recalling the bad experience with gas canisters at The Western Company, I asked, "What would happen if a bottle dropped and the neck snapped off?"

There were two schools of thought. The first, which I believed, was that the bottle would behave like an inflated balloon whose neck was released, launched like a rocket by the high-pressure helium. The other, led by a senior mechanical engineer, believed that helium's small molecular weight would have insufficient mass to move the loaded five-pound bottle. The cost of "fail-safing" the manufacturing area for this risk was very high, so a test was in order, an original "Myth Busters" test.

We designed the test within a chain link enclosure, loading a gas bottle in a manifold to simulate a neck rupture. With video cameras rolling to document the results, at the last minute the skeptical mechanical engineer emptied a five pound bag of flour on the test fixture. He figured the bottle would just sit there as the helium emptied out, and he wanted proof that the gas had exited. We were all amazed when the burst

> When it comes to safety, you cannot afford to allow the person with the strongest personality to win. Data and scientific evidence is required to substantiate a critical decision.

disk was punched, and a cloud of flour enveloped the test area! The noise of 8,000 psi of helium exiting the neck of the bottle was impressive! The bottle emerged from the dust and went straight up, more than a hundred feet in the air before beginning to tumble. It landed downrange more than 100 yards.

It was truly an "Oh, s**t" moment. We quietly packed up our equipment and returned to the plant, where we immediately began designing a fully-automated assembly room, so no humans were exposed in case of an accident. "MythBusters" would have been proud.

Libyan Threat

On April 15, 1986, President Reagan ordered an attack on Libya in response to terrorism sponsored by that country. Watching news reports the evening of the attack, there were videos of a Libyan farmer holding pieces of a missile and shouting in outrage that the U.S. had killed his chickens. I recognized several pieces of Texas Instruments HARM Missile in the wreckage—one of which was a wing, and another the rocket motor housing. Even with the poor quality of the video, the lettering on the missile parts was discernible, and I was concerned.

At the time, I was Division Operations Manager and Site Manager for TI's Lewisville facility, so the next morning, I made my way to a HARM missile display. I confirmed that the chicken farmer was, indeed, holding pieces of a HARM missile that had been launched in the raid. Clearly painted on the outside of the rocket motor, was: "For warranty information, contact Texas Instruments, Highway 121, Lewisville, Texas 75067."

As I was digesting this, several HARM executives and managers walked up, and we discussed the potential ramifications of having an "in the clear" address on our missiles. We contacted the Navy and requested the address be removed, and the change was implemented immediately.

But the damage was already done. A few weeks later, we received information that Libya had dispatched terrorist teams to carry out attacks on our facility. We immediately responded with additional security measures for the site, and though we couldn't discuss anything publicly,

> **Assess threats and act quickly!**

some of our employees came to correct conclusions about the risks we were facing. We took a number of angry questions and demands, including suggestions that we install machine gun nests and mine fields around the site.

A month later, we received word that the threats had been eliminated, but we didn't let our guard down. Thanks to U.S. intelligence organizations and the FBI, we escaped the threats, and you can bet we were breathing a deeper sigh of relief every day that passed without an incident.

When it comes to the safety of your employees, take immediate action to reduce risk and protect them. Look for advice from law enforcement and fire department organizations, then take prudent action. Be sure you're well-documented on all you do, in case of an incident.

Construction Tragedy

When Vista Ridge Mall was under construction in Lewisville, Texas, a mile from Texas Instruments plant, there was a huge construction mess that we dealt with daily. On my way to work one morning, a radio news report described a construction accident that killed two construction workers and injured another. The workers were working below-ground in a large sewer pipe, and were overcome by some kind of gas. I was concerned, but I wasn't aware of any connection with our site.

Later that day, a city official, trailed by police and fire officers, came to the lobby of the plant and demanded to see the site manager. When I got there, the city official stuck his finger in my chest and said: "This morning two workers were killed in the sewer downstream of your facility, and we traced a deadly chemical to your facility. If that chemical is the cause of death for those two workers, we're coming for you, and you'll be charged with their deaths." Gulp! That got my attention.

The city investigators had analyzed the effluent in the pipe where the workers died, and found traces of MEK (methyl-ethyl-ketone), a nasty chemical used in electronics manufacturing. They tracked the chemical up the sewer line more than a mile directly to the effluent stream coming from our plant. Health Department officials jumped to the conclusion that by allowing MEK in the sewer system TI was guilty of a whole host of crimes, including manslaughter in the deaths of the construction workers.

Facilities personnel immediately went into the site sewers and tracked the source of the MEK to several labs, where engineering technicians—despite work rules that forbade disposing of chemicals in the sinks—were dumping dangerous chemicals down the city sewer. When the managers of the various organizations were contacted, they didn't seem concerned, basically giving a "boys will be boys" response. I took the prerogative out of their hands by immediately ordering all lab sinks in the facility disconnected. This was a serious problem for lab personnel, but since they and their managers didn't seem concerned about fixing the problem, we took immediate action to clean up their act. We put together a capital package for emergency installation of sumps to collect lab effluent, and pump it into large barrels to be disposed of as hazardous chemical waste, regardless of what was actually in them. Over the course of a year, we found that very little chemical waste was in the effluents, but

> For environmental issues, take aggressive corrective action and thoroughly document investigations and actions.

the shotgun approach was warranted until we could track down the specific sources of the chemicals and take action. Did I mention that the costs for all these extraordinary activities were charged directly against the budgets of the offending and unresponsive organizations?

The medical examiner determined that the cause of death of the workers was methane asphyxiation, which is a hazard in most sewers, and it's why workers are required to wear breathing protection any time they work in sewers. These workers *hadn't* been wearing breathing equipment, and they were overwhelmed by the methane. While MEK shouldn't have been in the drains, it was so diluted it was deemed not to be a risk or a contributing factor.

Over the months of investigations, findings, and corrective actions, we maintained open communications with city officials. I met with them routinely to ensure they were up to speed, and we were totally responsive to all their inquiries. Based on our quick, definitive, and open-book response, the city dropped any action against TI. But for months we sampled every drop of effluent coming from the labs to ensure the techs had learned their lesson and weren't dumping chemicals down the drain. Once the wastewater was consistently "clean," we reconnected a few of the benign sinks to the city sewer. Although no one was ever identified for dumping chemicals down the drains, we had our suspicions and left a number of their sinks permanently disconnected to ensure compliance.

Chapter Four

When in Rome

Whether on the other side of the negotiation table, or the other side of the world, understanding the culture of those with whom you're working is critical. When selling to, or buying from, others, you need to understand their motivations and priorities. Observing local customs is important in building relationships, and understanding the way in which they do business is critical. You should work to become a good observer of behavior, learning how to read body language. At the end of my career, I was pretty good at reading a room. Observing the participants, their "peckin' order," and their behavior relative to others served me very well. Within minutes, I could often read the room and understand where I was going to bump heads, where I would have support, and where I needed to influence people to move to my position. Don't ask me to describe how I did this; often it was as much a feeling as a specific "tell." Just as successful gamblers become very good at reading their opponents, you can develop that ability for use in your business dealings, both internal and external.

Whatever the cultural norms for your business acquaintances (and personal relationships), you would be well-advised to do your homework ahead of time, including cultural sensitivity courses to avoid unintended insults. The following are some personal situations that may be helpful.

Jury Foreman

Within the first six months of my career, I was called for jury duty in downtown Dallas, Texas. The first day, after waiting in the jury room for more than four hours, I was selected for a jury panel and went to a court-room, where we waited an hour for the lawyers and judge to show up. We underwent questioning by the attorneys for the purpose of choosing a jury. The defendants were three young people (two girls and a boy) charged with two crimes each: possession of drugs, and possession of drugs with the intent to sell. Both were felonies, but the "intent" charge was far more serious. I was the youngest person on the jury panel, with modestly long hair and dressed neatly in a suit.

Each defendant had his/her own attorney, and for every step of the process, every attorney in the courtroom had to have his say. I suppose I must have been viewed as acceptable to the defense, since I was close to the age of the defendants and had longer hair. I was probably accept-able to the prosecution because I worked at Texas Instruments, was well-dressed, clean-shaven, and well-educated. After all was said and done, I was selected as a jury member. However, the joke was on the defense, as they didn't realize I had no experience with, nor tolerance of, illegal drugs.

We heard the case over two days, with undercover cops recounting drug purchases from the defendants, as well as the details of the raid and arrests. The girls were in the apartment with a huge pile of drugs and paraphernalia when the cops kicked in the door and arrested them. The door was closed as the search occurred, and the male defendant walked in while cops were in the apartment. He was arrested and charged with the same felonies as the girls.

Defense lawyers did not present a single witness, so when the pros-ecution concluded, each side went straight to closing arguments. After that, the judge and lawyers recessed for several hours while we sat and twiddled our thumbs. Finally, the judge came back into court with the lawyers, and he gave instructions to the jury and sent us to the jury room.

Once in that small room, we sat down at a table and looked at one another without a clue as to what to do next.

I made the mistake of asking if we should elect a foreman, everyone agreed, and they immediately elected me for the job. It was stunning, since I was the youngest person in the room, had no experience with our judicial system, and had no idea how to lead deliberations. There were four older women on the jury, grandmother-types who took great pity on those poor girls. The female defendants cleaned-up nicely for the trial versus what they looked like in their mug shots. The older women likely wanted the girls to get off completely free, blaming the male defendant for the whole mess, living illicitly with two women and undoubtedly leading them astray. Another faction was the law and order group who had no tolerance for druggies. They were ready to convict instantly. Then there was the third faction, who wanted to analyze the evidence and testimony in great detail and debate the situation to death.

After hours of discussion, debate, and two trips back into the court room to ask questions, we took a straw vote and realized we were terribly split. We argued for a number of additional hours over two days and were headed for deadlock, when I suggested we look at each charge individually.

First the women. They were in the apartment, with the drugs in plain sight, and since they lived there, they were in possession of the drugs and didn't even try to tell us the drugs weren't theirs. So the women were guilty, right? Yes, on possession, but what about intent to sell? Yes, because of the huge quantity. OK, now the women were guilty on both counts. However, the man wasn't in the apartment when the cops arrived. He came in later, and although it was his apartment, the argument was that the girls may have been responsible for the drugs, and he may not have known about them. I don't think anyone actually bought that argument, but it came from one of the grandmothers who felt she'd been bullied into giving up on the girls. She now turned to the cute young boy to try to claim some success out of the situation.

In the end, to avoid deadlock, I suggested we compromise and find him guilty on possession, but not guilty on intent to sell. There was absolutely no logic to that suggestion, but after two days of going over the same arguments, the law and order group got guilty verdicts on all three defendants, the uncertain group came over to the guilty side, and the grandmothers felt they won something. It was a miscarriage of justice, since the man was likely more at fault than the women, but timing is everything, since he was five minutes late getting back to the apartment, and we were exhausted. It was a compromise in what should have been a slam dunk conviction.

I wrote up the verdicts on all six charges, and we summoned the bailiff. An hour later, everyone was rounded up and returned to the courtroom, we filed back into the jury box, and the judge asked for our verdict. I was really nervous, and I could tell there was surprise in the room that I was foreman, given my youth. I read our verdicts, one at a time, and I could tell there was confusion in the courtroom, "Guilty, Guilty, Guilty, Guilty, Guilty, Not Guilty." Huh???

Everyone in the courtroom had to be asking, "What are they thinking?" But we didn't have to answer any questions, except when the judge asked each of us if we were unanimous in our verdicts. I kept waiting for one of the grandmothers to scuttle our ship at the last minute, but none did. The judge asked the defendants if they wanted the jury to set sentencing, and all three lawyers jumped to their feet and asked the judge to handle sentencing. I guess they viewed us as more unpredictable than the judge would be. The judge thanked us for our service, set the sentencing date, and adjourned court. We were released from jury duty after a full week of civic service.

Why have I told you about this event? Because it was hugely instructive, giving me leadership experience at a time in my career when I was learning leadership skills. Finding common ground and compromise were added to the set of tools I've used my entire life. Learning to manage discussions and arguments, provide persuasion and reasoning, effectively address diverse priorities and agendas, and weave together a consensus agreement, all these were important tools for my "management quiver." Recognizing differences and motivations in others is an

> Trying to achieve perfect consensus can devolve into an endless pursuit of herding cats.

ability that served me very well. Once you understand why someone feels a particular way, you have a much better likelihood of bridging the gap to a resolution.

When presented with division, you can choose to join one of the factions, or mediate between them. Consensus may not be achievable, but after a reasonable time, after listening to the varying perspectives and trying to accommodate them, a decision is required, and at least everyone feels they had a say and were listened to.

Other Cultures in the Workplace

During Texas Instruments' HARM missile production ramp-up, we hired hundreds of assemblers, including a number of South Vietnamese refugees who immigrated to the U.S.A. when the Communists took over their country. Many were well-educated professionals in their native country, but in the U.S., they were refugees who struggled with the English language and American culture. To work for us, they had to have basic English and math competencies, verified by testing during the application process. We initially brought in a small number of the refugees, and they proved to be great employees, grateful to have a good job and benefits. They loved their new home, and worked hard to support their families and build a new life here.

One man struck a real chord in my emotions. He was a college-educated professional and Air Force pilot in Viet Nam, a proud man who appreciated his electronic assembly job. Mr. Nguyen came to my attention one day as I was talking to the shop supervisor and asked how our Vietnamese employees were doing. She was very complimentary, saying they were great workers who only needed to be shown a job once to repeat it flawlessly. But there were some cultural adjustments needed. When I asked what she meant, she pointed out Mr. Nguyen and told me, "One day last week, Mr. Nguyen wasn't feeling well, and he needed to use the restroom. But it wasn't break time, and he was afraid to leave his work station, so he stayed at his work sta-

> Help people get a leg up, and they will strive to prove your confidence in them.

tion and embarrassed himself." The supervisor asked me to talk to Mr. Nguyen, which I did.

Mr. Nguyen and I became friends, and when I learned of his role as a pilot in the war, my respect for him grew. At an open house, Mr. Nguyen proudly brought his family to meet me. He was especially proud of his son, who was graduating from college. Mr. Nguyen and his family, with assistance from their church, had succeeded in putting their son through college, where he earned a degree in electrical engineering. When I asked the son where he would work after finishing school, he was embarrassed to say he hadn't received any job offers. The next day, I made a few calls and arranged for him to have an interview at another TI plant. He was offered a job, which he gratefully accepted.

When I next saw Mr. Nguyen, you would have thought I was a saint. He presented me with a gift, a fine porcelain Vietnamese tea service with a small pot and cups. I was embarrassed that he was making such a big deal about it, but I wasn't about to refuse his beautiful gift. He explained the significance of the pottery and its painted scene, and I have the tea set to this day. Every time I saw Mr. Nguyen, he would proudly tell me how well his son was doing. I remember Mr. Nguyen fondly for his humble spirit, pride in his family, commitment and hard work, and service to our country.

While we are often quick to assume the universal virtue of American culture, we can learn much from other cultures. Work accommodations are sometimes needed to enable good workers to become great. Just be fair and supportive, knowing and respecting your people as individuals.

Visiting Japan

In the mid-1980s, two senior Texas Instruments managers and I made a trip to Japan to learn about Japanese manufacturing and quality processes. At that time, Japan was a powerful manufacturing force, and learning from them was in order. My mentor, Jim Houlditch, put together a fantastic trip, although he didn't accompany us. Jim had been S.V.P. of Quality for TI's global Semiconductor Business, and he had a free hand to tackle world-wide quality improvement. So when Jim called the President of TI Japan to put on a good trip for us, he got results. We received outstanding support, hosted by Shin Okhura, V.P. of Quality and Productivity for TI Japan. He traveled with us during the two weeks we were in Japan as guide and interpreter. We visited two TI sites and a number of TIJ's customers and suppliers, gaining special access to their executives and plant managers to learn Japanese manufacturing and quality technologies. It was a fascinating trip from many perspectives, and the lessons learned have stayed with me my entire life.

Personal Responsibility Returning to Tokyo one afternoon, we were delayed at a train station due to a strong thunderstorm in the area. The delay was unusual, as Japanese public services run on time. It was unavoidable due to weather, an act of God. Nevertheless, the stationmaster loudly

> Apology isn't defeat. It shows you see your mistake and will work to fix it.

opened the door to his office above the station platform, and marched ramrod stiff down the stairs to the platform, his three-piece suit immaculately buttoned and his shirt still crisp and white. At the bottom of the stairs, he bowed deeply, rose and announced something, then he bowed deeply and held his position in a stance of profound shame to everyone on the platform. Shin told us he had announced with great embarrassment and humility that the train was delayed, apologizing profusely for the delay. All part of the Japanese culture of respect and personal accountability.

WHEN IN ROME

Visiting Japanese Customers The customer/supplier hierarchy is highly structured in Japan, and when we—representing a supplier—visited a customer, it was like the customer sat on a throne with us at his feet. After initial introductions, things became more cordial, and several executives were friendly, having spent time in the U.S.A. and understanding our informal business customs. One customer had a burr under his saddle due to a TI-caused delivery delay six months earlier, and he was brutal. As soon as we entered, we had no more than shaken hands and exchanged business cards than he launched into an aggressive, deep-throated scolding of the entire TI team. Of course, we couldn't understand a word, but watching Shin, bowing and taking a whipping, and expressing regret for causing the customer problems, we could tell the discussion wasn't going well. After the lambasting was over and the customer was satisfied we had eaten enough humble pie, he lightened up, and we had a conversation. The beginning of the meeting was terrible, but it reinforced the cultural aspects of doing business in Japan.

> Fully understand your customer when you're being criticized. Hear what is being said and go to work to fix the problem, even if it's only perception.

Japanese Culture Later in my career I had the opportunity to take a cultural sensitivity course while in China on a business trip. The focus was on Asian business norms, and I learned that I had unknowingly insulted the Japanese on my earlier visits. For instance, when meeting a Japanese person for the first time, you are expected to make a small bow if the person is a peer, customer, or socially-acceptable person. Presenting your business card is to be done respectfully, with both hands, facing the person directly. You are expected to read his card carefully, giving respect to the card as a representation of the person and worthy of respect. Americans typically hand out their cards one handed, or toss them informally on the conference table, insulting Japanese visitors.

Giving gifts is a mark of respect in Japanese culture, and the complexity of the wrapping represents the degree of respect with which you

> Before traveling to another culture, take the time to learn its customs.

hold the recipient. As the gift is unwrapped, the recipient quietly oohs, aahs, and nods sagely when each fold is revealed. The recipient thanks the giver profusely and gratefully acknowledges not only the gift, but also the beauty and intricacy of the wrapping.

We had brought TI pen and pencil sets as gifts for the people we visited. The first problem was that everyone had pen and pencil sets that they gave to *lower-level visitors*, so we insulted them with poor gifts. Second, they weren't wrapped. Third, we didn't use glowing terms nor bows when we presented the gifts. We were ugly Americans, for sure.

Our worst gaff, though, was what we did to our guide and interpreter, Shin Okhura. Shin had devoted two weeks to us, as well as weeks of work leading up to our arrival, so he invested a lot in our trip. We thought we would honor Shin with a nice gift the last day, so we went to a liquor store and bought bottles of Chivas Regal and Jack Daniels whiskeys. Whiskeys were very expensive in Japan, so the gifts were nice enough, but we didn't wrap them. Instead, we carried them around the whole day in the plastic bags from the liquor store, clinking as we walked through the day. We made a nice speech for Shin, thanking him for his hard work on our behalf, then handed him the plastic bags. No wrapping; just shopping bags. He opened the bags and nodded appreciatively, but we could tell he wasn't ecstatic. Sorry, Shin, you deserved better.

Before traveling to another culture, make it a priority to learn the customs of the people you will be interacting with. It will save you and your hosts a lot of embarrassment. Cultural sensitivity courses are worth the investment.

Patent Dispute Texas Instruments invented and patented the integrated circuit in the U.S. In the early 1960s, and in 1963, TI filed for a Japanese patent. For years, the Japanese government delayed action on TI's patent requests until Japanese electronics companies had developed a semiconductor industry, based in part on stolen technology. Japanese companies and government invested in semiconductor technology for years, until the majority of the largest producers in the world were Japanese. *Thirty years later,* the

> International experience is invaluable for understanding the expectations of your customers and suppliers.

Japanese government finally issued TI's patent, but by then, the damage was done.

Open markets and free trade are good for everyone, but the playing field needs to be as level as possible. Burying your head in the sand with trade barriers is self-defeating. You must learn to succeed with international competitors, despite sometimes-unfair disadvantages.

When Corporations and School Boards Meet

In the mid-1980's, I was asked by State Senator Jane Nelson of Lewisville to represent the region on the State of Texas Long Range Education Planning Task Force to help develop a vision for the future of education in the State of Texas. Texas Instruments supported me and funded my travel expenses, so I went to Austin, briefed by Ms. Nelson's staff and TI's PR group, bright-eyed and full of naïve expectations of helping the kids of Texas. What a rude awakening I received. I was one of forty people convened from around the state, representing school districts, universities, state government, and business. The task force was comprised of twenty teachers, a few university professors, state education administrators, school principals, school board members and superintendents, and two business people—one of whom was me.

We were briefed by task force sponsors and state administrators, and a chairperson was appointed to moderate the committee. We met in Austin five times over four months, and it was apparent from the beginning that the school contingent's only objective was more funding, while dismissing other points of view. Task force minutes were biased and staff was unwilling to make changes, even when I requested a correction when I was misquoted.

At our first task force meeting, one after another of the teachers ran rough-shod over anyone who didn't share their views. District Superintendents, Board members, and others tried to speak, only to be shouted down by the loud-mouthed bullies. Late in the first meeting, I decided I needed to speak up for the customers of Texas' public school districts: businesses, universities, and organizations who depend on the product of our schools.

TI's experience was that many high school graduates couldn't read at a sixth grade level and basic math was a challenge. This was before the days of norm-based testing, and I wanted to introduce the concepts of fundamental competency and testing, and teacher and school accountability. Mustering my courage and diplomatic skills, I spent a minute talking about the challenges the business community faced in finding competent entry-level employees. When I mentioned failures in standards and lack of accountability to teach to those standards, you would have thought I had poured gasoline on a fire. I was shouted down and personally attacked, scorned because I was completely ignorant of "the real world," and told to grab a pencil and come to one of their class rooms to get a real education. OK, so I hadn't been in a class room in years, and I hadn't walked in those teachers' shoes, but I knew what it took to be successful in any endeavor: setting clear expectations, providing sufficient assets and resources, measuring progress, and holding people accountable.

When I put that on the table, it got really loud in the conference room, and some of the teachers lectured me, blaming everyone and everything else for the lack of success in their schools. This was enormously discouraging for someone who really wanted to help. After the first session when I had my head handed to me, I just checked the box. I put in the time and carried out my responsibilities, but I was hopeless. Today the report is languishing on dusty shelves all over the state. Years later, state and federal governments began facing up to these issues and passed legislation trying to address some of the problems. In some cases, the solutions haven't worked well, in some cases they've added bureaucracy without benefitting students, and in some cases they've gotten it right but been shouted down. Yet, there are examples of successes in school districts all over

> In some cases, you may not be able to bridge the culture gap.

the country because principals and teachers refused to lower their standards, and because school districts are reformed by passionate people with high expectations for students, despite their backgrounds or economic circumstances.

Entertaining the Japanese

Sometimes you get to show other people your culture. Such was the case in early 1992 in my role as General Manager of Texas Instruments' Enterprise Systems Division. We were visited by twelve members of a business development team from Kobe Steel, one of the largest companies in Japan and a member of Japan's inner circle of power brokers. Following its start in the steel industry, Kobe branched out into other areas, and their visit was to explore teaming opportunities for our companies. Two other TI managers and I hosted the Japanese throughout their visit to the U.S., and we called in managers from across TI to represent other areas of interest. Kobe's team leader, whom I'll call Koji, was a fifty-five-ish executive, who spoke limited English. Other team members were younger, but only three spoke English well enough to converse. We planned a dinner one evening at The Trail Dust restaurant in Dallas, picking the group up at their hotel in a bus for the thirty-minute trip to the restaurant. Our dinner party numbered about twenty, and the bus ride to The Trail Dust was quiet. Our guests knew nothing of what they were about to experience.

The Trail Dust was a pure-Texas cowboy restaurant with excellent steaks and an atmosphere that was a large part of the fun. Diners sat at long, rustic wooden tables, and the walls were decorated with cowboy paraphernalia and Texas artwork. The restaurant featured a wooden dance floor in the center, surrounded by second floor balconies above. That night the music was played by a DJ at high volume, and the repertoire was pure country.

Ties were not permitted at The Trail Dust. The servers make a big show of marching to the table with sheers to cut the tie off any patron foolish enough to wear one. The cut tie is then hammered onto the wall with the person's business card—the walls were decorated with hundreds of them. We brought sacrificial ties for everyone in the party, and during the bus ride the Japanese were puzzled when their ties were replaced with our ugly ones.

When we arrived, I took a minute to visit with the manager and explain that we wanted a real Texas show for our Japanese guests, and he assured me with a smile he could handle the challenge. We were led on a long walk around the dance floor to the opposite side of the restaurant, and by now the Japanese had gotten the idea this was going to be a little looser evening than they anticipated. Each visitor had a camera, and by the time the evening was over, they had shot more than 100 photos each and were begging for more film. The waitresses, in fine Texas form, swooped in, exposing lots of bodily real estate, and flirting shamelessly with the Japanese. Our visitors immediately began drinking heavily, although they all remained upright the entire evening. When the waitresses ceremoniously brought out the sheers and began cutting off ties, it was like a presidential press conference, with non-stop camera flashes. Each Kobe exec, after his tie was severed, jumped to his feet with upraised arms, screamed something in Japanese, grabbed the hammer and nails, and pounded his tie and business card to the wall. The rest of the diners in the restaurant were watching the show, clearly amused.

After several rounds of drinks and happy toasts, it was time to order dinner, and each of the Japanese wanted the largest steak on the menu, along with appetizers and extras of all sorts. When the enormous steaks arrived, the Kobe execs looked daunted, but in the end they were up to the challenge.

After the main course, I went to the restroom, then stopped off at the gift shop to buy mementoes for the Japanese. By the time I returned to the table, it had been more than twenty minutes, and the Kobe contingent was gone. So were the other TI hosts, and I experienced a moment of panic, thinking perhaps everyone had decided to call it a night and headed to the bus. I shouldn't have worried.

As I approached the dance floor, I saw a large group of diners surrounding it, watching what was going on in the middle. At one end was a two-story, stainless steel slide curving steeply down from the second floor balcony to the dance floor. The Kobe execs were gathered at the bottom of the slide on the dance floor. Koji was on the second floor at the top of the slide. He was immaculate in his buttoned, three-piece suit, with his cut-off tie stub still neatly knotted. Cameras were firing non-stop as he stepped to the top of the slide, raised his hands high above his head, and screamed, *"Banzai!"* In response, all the Japanese below reciprocated his yell. I was amazed so few Japanese could make so much noise, until I realized that everyone else in the restaurant was also yelling, "Banzai!" The Kobe execs were so good-natured, joking and having such fun, that the American customers were laughing and joining in. Koji went through the Banzai ritual three times, each time gaining a louder response from the entire restaurant, then he jumped straight up in the air, landing on his butt on the top of the slide. He accelerated down the slick stainless steel, and shot out onto the dance floor with enough velocity to slide across its entire length on his behind. When he ran out of speed, he flopped on his back, laughing uncontrollably, and everyone joined in. Hilarious!

Of course, the rest of the Kobe team had to have their turns, and then commenced thirty minutes of "Banzai" slides, to the accompaniment of flashing cameras and gales of laughter. The hilarious "Banzai bedlam" went down in the history of great international relations.

At last it was time to leave, and we rounded up our troops and headed for the bus. Each of the Japanese had to visit the gift shop, and multiple remembrances were purchased. At least once, we escorted our visitors back to the bar so they could reload. I paid the massive bill, and after herding the crew onto the bus, we sat down for the ride to the hotel. Not quite so much decorum this time, though. They were all still wearing the stubs of their ties, although their suits

> Allow time for entertainment with customers and employees. It's great for building relationships.

were by now askew. I handed out mementoes to each of the Kobe execs, and there was much bowing, and, "Aah, Stewart-san, what a wonderful evening."

The Competitive Landscape

Sometimes a culture change occurs from within. That what's happened as I was sitting in a Texas Instruments' conference room in 1988, meeting with a number of executives, including Jerry Junkins, Chairman, President, and CEO. Jerry was a visionary, and he was speaking of the impending demise of the USSR and the transition of the Defense Industry from a victor over the Iron Curtain to a peacetime Defense market. He commented on the swinging pendulum of America's federal spending from defense-heavy to social-heavy budgets, and his view was that TI must become more competitive to survive in a shrinking Defense market. The discussion turned to unfair trading barriers erected by Japan and other countries, and his perspective was truly visionary, changing my view forever. Jerry's comments centered on the huge benefits of competition; the concept of sharpening yourself constantly against the best in the world. Companies that succeed in the global marketplace, irrespective of the barriers erected against them, are unstoppable. His message: "Who cares what barriers they put against us; we'll find a way to excel, year after year, country after country, challenge after challenge, for the success of our stakeholders." That message changed my view of competition, the global landscape, and the determination to overcome whatever confronts us. We must fight to win in the global marketplace, fair or unfair, where our true value is determined by our customers.

> Companies that succeed in the global marketplace, irrespective of the barriers erected against them, are unstoppable.

Competition is a good thing, and if we constantly strive to improve against the best in the world, never resting on our laurels, and overcoming barriers, we have the opportunity to be global winners. Should we work for level playing fields? Sure. But we don't let unfair trading practices defeat us.

Community Involvement

During my years at Texas Instruments in Lewisville, Texas, from 1983 to 1989, there were amazing challenges and opportunities, lasting friendships, and zany and outlandish work assignments that made life interesting. As Lewisville Site Manager, one of my duties was to represent TI's 5,000 employees to the community, at a time when TI was changing from a closed company to one with a positive public image. My community activities helped employee pride and our image in the community. Public perception is a benefit that helps local relations, employee recruiting, and stock valuation, and I worked to be out-front with communications.

For several years, I worked with Lewisville Mayor Ann Pomykal, and we had a good relationship. When she decided not to run for re-election, we discussed bringing her to TI as our Community Relations Advocate. This had never been done at TI, but I received support from the executive team, and it turned out to be one of the best hires I ever made. Ann helped us (me) polish our (my) image and make meaningful investments in the community. Working as a spokesperson for the company, we originated and carried out projects that elevated our standing in the community and helped make TI a popular place to work. We sup-

> Don't be shy about expanding your role outside the walls of your company.

ported the community with open houses, United Way leadership, donations, and community and charitable events. I felt we really made a difference in the community. I recommend becoming involved in your community; it's rewarding, and you'll expand your network of valuable contacts while you help improve your company's image.

Talking at Cross-Purposes

In 1989, I moved from Texas Instruments' Defense Business to its Information Technology Business to head up the newly-formed Enterprise Systems Business. As I dug into the challenges of my new job, I knew significant organizational work was required, since the groups I inherited were very diverse. I toured a number

> Just because you're in charge doesn't mean your employees will do what you ask/tell them to do.

of TI's global sites early in my new assignment, and felt as if I was an alien. I stood in front of hundreds of my employees to communicate my priority for customer support, gauging our success by meeting our customers' expectations. That was foreign to these IT folks, who often set priorities based on what they were interested in, rather than on things their customers cared about. I suggested they should satisfy their customers *first*, move research projects to *second priority*, and *cut costs* dramatically. The people in the organization viewed me as an outsider, a manufacturing grunt who was clueless when it came to IT processes and technologies. At best I received lip service from the organization. After all, under prior management, they got pretty much everything they asked for.

Intentional Change of Management Style

One of my early goals had been to become an executive at an early age, a goal I didn't achieve until I learned to control my volatile personality. The intentional changes I made in the beginning of my career had served me well as a supervisor and young manager. I became an aggressive leader, hard-driving and sometimes intolerant of failure. FSI International was where I executed another intentional change, away from a "take no prisoners" style, learning to respond with more tact, patience, and a congenial personality. It took me far too long to learn the lessons of diplomacy, and though I progressed quickly from supervision to large-organization management, I was self-limited for too long.

> Let your talented people exercise their abilities and potentials, supporting your vision, rather than trying to control everything personally.

FSI International's executive team had a different management style than I grew up with. The culture was "softer" than Texas Instruments, and FSI was where I learned that not everyone worked sixty-hour weeks. CEO Joel Elftmann was a role model for me at this point in my career—calmer and more caring, while still a good leader. FSI was where I learned it's more enjoyable to let talented people exercise their abilities and potentials, supporting a common vision, rather than to try to control everything. I also learned that there's nothing wrong with taking customers out for a round of golf or a hunting trip, or enjoying a reciprocal trip. My family will tell you that this was a time when I also changed significantly as a person, husband, and father.

In a Pig's Ear

In 2012, at the end of my time with Schneider Electric, I had planned a hunting weekend at our ranch, planning to leave early Friday to head to the ranch. Unfortunately, the boss called a meeting for early Friday morning, and I "attended" by phone. A new CFO—Sebastien Chaque from France—had recently arrived on the scene, and he was on the call. After the boss and others on the call gave me a hard time

> While practical jokes can be fun, beware the Jedi master who can flip the joke on you.

about hunting pigs, Sebastien piled on with a funny comment about bringing him a hog. At that point, I decided it was time to welcome Sebastien to Wayne's World!

The weekend was successful, and I killed a large sow from which I cut one of the ears. I stuck the gross, hairy, stinky hog's ear in a freezer bag and put it on ice. We had an early meeting on Monday, and I put the ear in a Victoria's Secret gift bag and covered it with tissue paper. The executive team gathered in the president's office for the meeting, and when Sebastien arrived, I made a short speech about bringing something suitable back from the weekend. He sat with a half-smile on his face, not knowing how to take my sense of humor. When I handed him the Victoria's Secret bag, he looked at it apprehensively, then lifted out the tissue paper until he could see the freezer bag, where the large, hairy, stinky, ugly, bloody hog's ear resided. When he pulled the bag out, everyone in the room groaned, then the laughter volume took off, and I was enjoying the situation.

Sebastien, the ultimate Frenchman, one-upped me by saying, "Oh, this is great, I think I could eat this." Everything went weird at that point. He said there were specialty restaurants in France that served pig's ears and other porcine delicacies. He definitely turned the tables on me. A while later when I ran into Sebastien in the hall, I asked him for the ear so I could use it on someone else. Sebastien once again bested me when he said, "No, I have it in my office, and you can't have it. I'm going to re-gift it."

Golfing with the Executive Team

I love to play golf, but I'm not very good at it. I've had a few good rounds, but mostly I shoot in the 80s with an occasional foray into the 70s. Far too often, I soar into the 90s, leaving me embarrassed. My first golfing experience with the Schneider Electric U.S. executive group was an invitation in 2007 from President Dean Meyer to play a round at his club, along with V.P.s Bob Klein and Jeff Drees. Dean and Jeff were very good golfers, usually shooting in the 70s or low 80s, and, while Bob was distance-challenged, he could chip and putt, lights-out.

On this first golf day with SE executives, less than two months after joining the company, I was paired with Jeff Drees, and to say he enjoys gambling while golfing is an understatement. While getting ready to play off the first tee, they were setting up the bets, a game I didn't know. Best I recall, it was eight points per hole, with each point worth 25¢, and every hole worth $2. Then things got really crazy. Every time someone yelled, "Press!" the point value doubled. If one of the players felt he had an advantage, he would yell, "Press!" and all values doubled from that point on. Not to be outdone, Jeff and Dean both viewed presses as a matter of manly pride, and they weren't going to be outdone by anyone.

As I stepped up to the first tee, my partner, Jeff, yelled, "Press!" No one had ever seen me swing a golf club before, so Jeff's press was a brash act of machismo. After questioning Jeff's sanity, I hit my tee shot in the fairway, but with no spectacular result. Then commenced the craziest round of golf I've ever been associated with. The advantage changed on every hole, and the bets doubled at least five times. When we arrived at the 16th tee, Jeff and I were ahead, and Jeff teed off first. He hit a mighty blast, far, far out of bounds. Undeterred, he immediately yelled, "Press!"

I stepped to the tee and hit a good shot on the par five, and we headed down the fairway. Jeff thought it was funny, but by now the per-hole value was north of $100, Jeff was out of the hole, and it was all up to me. I made a couple of good shots and finished with a par, which won the hole. Jeff was ecstatic, claiming responsibility for winning the hole, since he was wise enough to press when he knew I was going to step up. We went to 17, which we lost, and on 18, we tied. After being up and down by more than $100, Jeff and I finished with a $10 win. How in the world all

> If you're going to work with executives—especially sales folks—you'd better be ready to play on their terms.

that turmoil, confusion, and mayhem came out that evenly, I have no idea. But we won, thanks in no small part to Jeff's ridiculous aggressiveness.

After the round, while settling up the bets, I had an inspiration. When Dean paid off his bet with a $10 bill, I had him sign it. Thus began a tradition that lasted the rest of my time at SE. Every time I golfed with the SE guys, I'd have the losers autograph my winnings. I never spent any of those bills, and when I retired, I had a cache of signed bills in my wallet. It was great fun, since any time someone started talking golf smack, I'd reach in my pocket and pull out the stack of bills with all those autographs. When I read the names and values of the payoffs, the verbal antagonist usually slunk away from the competitive field of smack-talk. When I retired from SE, good friend Bob Klein presented me a framed shadow box, with a golfer at the bottom and a title at the top, "Game On." He included a signed $1 bill with retirement congratulations, and when I got home, it took only a few minutes to pull my winnings from my wallet and pin them into the framed shadow box. What a great retirement gift, it hangs in a place of honor in my study, and I hope to add to it with more winnings from my friend, Bob.

Chapter Five

Intentional Quality

Quality is an intentional, unending commitment to being the best you possibly can be. But until the people of your organization recognize that their professional quality commitment is inextricably a part of their personal quality ethic, you run the risk of quality failures and backtracking. Ethics, integrity, quality, and character are all part and parcel of a quality life. Your values define you, and character is the "lived-out" expression of those values over a period of years, to the point that people are confident they can depend on you to consistently do the right thing. Following are a few stories of my quality walk, beginning with the need to make an intentional decision to balance my work and personal lives.

Quality Evolution

Texas Instruments was always on the forefront of manufacturing excellence due to its advanced technologies and quality systems. In the early 1980s, in advance of the arrival of the plethora of quality gurus, TI crafted its own quality systems, adopting outside techniques and inventing its own processes and systems when nothing in industry filled the bill. TI's embrace of manufacturing excellence evolved into a comprehensive quality culture that resulted in outstanding products and a number of prestigious quality awards over the years.

Quality is first and foremost a way of life, beginning with respect for people and your profession, ethical behavior, solid credibility, and constructive speech. When your employees see you living a quality life-style and expecting the best from yourself and them, they will respond positively.

A New Perspective on Quality

Will Willoughby was a quality icon within NASA, leading its quality and reliability program during its years of lunar expeditions, and later with the U.S. Navy, providing quality leadership for its Materiel Command. It was in his capacity as the Navy's quality assurance executive that I met Will in the mid-1980s when we hosted him for tours of Texas Instruments' HARM Missile Facility.

On one visit, Will gave an impactful speech to our employees. He was one of those people who gave us hell every time he visited, but he spent a lot of time with us because he knew we were deeply committed to quality, and he wanted to help us because he saw potential in us. Will said some things during that speech I've never forgotten. He began by describing the priorities of his life:

1. God
2. Country
3. Family.

Many years later, he's still having an impact on me. His speech dealt with an individual's commitment to quality, and he began by observing that he found a cigarette butt on the sidewalk leading to the front door of our facility. He told us the person who dropped that cigarette butt should not be a part of the HARM program, because that person didn't have a commitment to quality.

You can imagine the audience at this point questioning where Will was going with this. As he spoke, it became clear that there was no such thing as work quality separate from personal quality. If one is committed to quality, then that commitment applies to all aspects of his life. A person fully-committed to quality could no more throw a cigarette butt on the sidewalk than he could allow a defect in a HARM missile. It was likely Will was using a bit of hyperbole in his speech, but I have never forgotten his words. I think there is truth in what he said, and I learned from, and accepted, his challenge.

During the 1980s, TI's Defense Business was successful in raising the expectations for, and delivery of, quality in all its products and services. An article from *Aviation Week & Space Technology*, the "bible" of the defense and aerospace industry, reported that TI was recognized for its quality progress, with its HARM production facility recognized as an "Exemplary Facility" by the Navy.

> Quality begins with a mindset of relentless and continual improvement.

As Will carried out his quality mission within the Navy and the industries that supported it, he began holding TI up as his standard. On several occasions he sent other Defense contractors to see and learn from us, saying, "You need to go see Texas Instruments. They're doing it right, and you should learn from them." Over the years, I hosted a number of competitors in our facility for tours and briefings, and I was asked to travel twice to competitors' facilities to advise them on quality. Interesting, isn't it, that while we were working so hard to improve our own deficiencies, we were being held up as a standard. I didn't feel comfortable in that role, given some of the issues we dealt with on a daily basis.

In 1988, Senator Sam Nunn, Chairman of the Senate Armed Services Committee, visited TI, and we briefed and toured him through the HARM facility. He was highly complementary of what we'd accomplished, and it was gratifying to be recognized for our years of hard work. TI's commitment to quality and reliability ultimately resulted in winning the 1992 Malcolm Baldrige National Quality Award, the first Defense contractor to receive that prestigious designation.

Your core values define you; there is no way to escape them, although you can at times make mistakes. When people know they can depend on you to do the right things, make the right decisions, support the right standards and the people who live them, you'll be recognized as the type person who can effectively lead a high-performance organization.

Cost Reduction as a Way of Life

Labor learning curves improve at 85–90 percent rates under normal conditions, meaning every time production quantity doubles, the labor content goes down by 15-10 percent, respectively. Adding the effects of production volumes, tooling and test equipment investment, design changes, new production techniques, and quality improvements, at Texas Instruments we challenged our teams to achieve improvement curves of 75–85 percent. These goals yielded a ten point labor improvement over conventional electronics assembly operations. Since TI preferred firm fixed price (FFP) contracts, the risks and rewards were 100 percent on us, and we executed programs with aggressive improvements on multiple fronts. Across more than ten years of Paveway production history, the improvement curve actually approached 70 percent. Lest anyone get the idea this was a windfall for TI, every year of improvements resulted in lowered pricing for all future years, since cost data was open and available to the DoD during subsequent negotiations. The Air Force loved us, and it was a great deal for the U.S. taxpayer, getting lowered pricing, year after year.

> The status quo is never good enough.

Every day, you should seek out and implement improvements in your performance, challenging your teams, and unleashing their creative powers. Not all initiatives will be successful, but mistakes and failures made while positively pushing the envelope can be corrected. When mistakes were made in my organization, I "picked up" my folks, dusted them off, and encouraged them to try again.

Managing Operations

In 1994, when I joined FSI International and took over Global Operations, I found immature processes and largely subjective measures of quality and operational excellence. There were no product- or process-specific measures of quality. Manufacturing processes were not benchmarked relative to competitors, and customer satisfaction was purely anecdotal. We quickly began launching measures of product quality, process capability, and customer satisfaction.

My work at Texas Instruments had taught me the need for five fundamental Key Performance Indicators (KPIs) for products and underlying processes: customer satisfaction, quality, time, and cost. True for any industry and operation, I recommend challenging yourself to measure your operation's success based on the following.

> How do you know if you're winning, if you don't keep score?

First, customer satisfaction must be measured. Back then, customer surveys were in their infancy, so we used product returns and service calls to measure how well we were satisfying our customers. Today, the science of customer satisfaction has been revolutionized, and some say we've gone overboard to the point of "survey exhaustion," but it's necessary as the primary measure of quality.

Second, quality must be measured at the output of the manufacturing processes. The measures must evaluate product capabilities for their intended purposes, utilizing measures that matter to the customers.

Third, time-based measures of the underlying processes are needed, including cycle time, lead time, and on-time delivery performance.

Fourth, costs need to be measured for assessing both budget performance and continuous improvement. Argument could be made that cost is a function of the other KPIs, and that's true, but I preferred to measure costs in addition to the other parameters. Annual budget and cost improvement goals and plans should be implemented.

The last (fifth) KPI deals with product and process capability compared to competitors and/or industry "best in class." This one is easier to say than to implement, since many competitive benchmarks are considered proprietary. Sometimes, this has to take the form of market share comparisons.

Objective process and product metrics/KPIs must be put in place. If they don't exist, you're flying blind.

Timeliness Is A Priority

I've always felt that timeliness was a virtue, and late arrival at an appointment or meeting is disrespectful of others. Sometimes it's inevitable, but you should call to provide an estimated arrival time so others may decide whether to proceed or wait. In addition to arriving on time, I've always tried to finish meetings on time, to respect others' calendars. This comes under the heading of "do what you say, and say what you do," building credibility.

> Applying humor to a recurrent disciplinary problem can sometimes result in team building.

While at TI in the 90s, in response to the irritating late-arrival behaviour from several of my managers, I originated a simple way to impress on my team the priority for timeliness: I implemented a "tardiness fine system" for staff meetings. Anyone arriving late paid a fine of $1 per minute, to a maximum of $5. The money went into a party fund for a team get-together. A sergeant-at-arms was appointed as time keeper and fine collector, a treasurer held the funds and provided financial reports, and the entire team comprised the Kangaroo Court to hear appeals. Younger team members were appointed to these positions, since they enjoyed the notoriety and recognition of taking money from more senior managers. If someone felt unfairly fined, he/she was free to appeal to the Kangaroo Court, and the Court had the option of eliminating the fine, adjusting it, or levying additional fines. Pretty quickly everyone realized an appeal was pointless, and maybe even dangerous, since the Court was likely to impose additional fines for wasting the time of the Court.

Not surprisingly, on-time arrival at meetings became the norm, since the harassment factor for late arrival could be intense. One of our senior managers was genetically incapable of arriving anywhere on time, and he would often arrive as much as twenty minutes late. He endured good-natured joshing for a while, but it wasn't long before a sharp undercurrent emerged. He became so frustrated one day that he pulled a $100 bill out of his wallet and threw it on the table, stating, "Here, I'm pre-paying my fines. Let me know when this runs out." I think he was actually mad, but we didn't give him his money back.

I wasn't immune, and when the boss was late, everyone piled on. I was held to the strictest of deadlines, and the Kangaroo Court enjoyed creating additional punishments for me. I was generally the first one fined, and I rarely appealed, since I knew what the answer would be.

Start-Up Board Assignment

In 2003, I was invited by a friend to sit on the Board of Directors of his new company, when he and his partner bought the assets of their prior employer. It was a small and risky venture from the beginning, but there were a few existing customers, and the owners went to work trying to find new customers, while providing

> As a board member, your primary responsibility is a fiduciary one to the stakeholders of the company.

support for their existing customer base. The President was skillful at finding investors, and he invited Dick Ivey and me to join his Board. We met routinely as a Board for a year or so, to advise the owners, but before long, they began focusing on sales and lost interest in "minding the store." Financial reporting became sporadic, Board meetings declined, and for several years the company barely survived. When its cash problems worsened, the owners weren't able to earn enough to live on, and they soon became desperate. After going for more than five years without a Board meeting, one was called in 2011, looking for our help. We re-opened Board activities, and began advising the owners on how best to realize value from their investment. The President didn't pursue our recommendations, and the company continued to decline. He continued to look to us to support him, yet he failed to follow our direction. His investors were on course to lose one hundred percent of their investments, and I felt unable to fulfill my fiduciary duty to the stakeholders. I couldn't in good conscience be a part of the company's mismanagement, and I resigned from the Board. Dick Ivey resigned shortly thereafter, and the company went under without generating any value or returning anything on investor capital.

Telling the Boss No

As with many start-ups, FSI International's founder Joel Elftmann owned the headquarters facility, leasing it to FSI. The transaction is typically an investment by the founder that guarantees a long-term tenant on preferential terms. The lease came up for renewal not long after I arrived, and I was faced with handling a "related party transaction." Public companies are required to handle those transactions at arms-length, as market-based transactions. I had the responsibility to ensure FSI was getting a good deal.

> Always conduct yourself with integrity, refusing to deal in areas of questionable ethics. Don't blindside anyone (your boss!), but stand your ground.

Tobin Real Estate was FSI's corporate real estate advisor, and Bill Tobin was a first-class real estate professional. I asked Bill to perform a market analysis of comparable facilities in the area. He found that the rental price on FSI's HQ building was somewhat higher than market pricing. Bill recommended new pricing, and he handled the delicate discussions with Joel. To his credit, Joel agreed to give the company a market-based lease, resolving audit issues and ensuring FSI wouldn't have to relocate to another facility. I was happy to sign the new lease, saving the company money, even though my boss was grumpy with me for a while.

Chapter Six

Dealing with Big Personalities

There are people in this world who are larger than life, and others who are so focused on "ruling the roost" that they are overbearing and arrogant. Sometimes, they can be outright dangerous, and many feel fulfilled only when they belittle others. Tread lightly, but firmly, because once stepped on without response, you will be branded with a weakness label, whether true or not.

She Did What?

At the beginning of my career, Texas Instruments' Paveway Laser Guided Bomb assembly area housed more than 100 assemblers who were skilled at soldering, assembling, and testing high-tech electronic systems. Many were women who sat at work stations on "the line," a succession of manufacturing tables with kit boxes and work instructions arrayed in front of them. Each assembler received work from an upstream operation, performed her function on the work in process, then passed it along to the downstream station. These women knew their jobs and were highly skilled, producing exceptionally high-quality defense systems.

The people I supervised were far more experienced than I, and having a low-key personality was a benefit, recognizing that I didn't know it all but was willing to learn from others—I wanted to learn from them. I enjoyed sitting next to the assemblers and asking them how they did their jobs, and they not only respected me for asking, but they enjoyed teaching me.

DEALING WITH BIG PERSONALITIES

Some of those women could be really crusty. They were typically in their thirties and forties, earning a good living supporting their families. When they got to the weekend, many of them could really party, and they came to work on Mondays with experiences to relate to the other women on the line. While working, they talked with

> You must find a way to manage unseemly behavior without becoming part of it, or a target.

one another across a 20,000 square foot area, and never missed a beat. They often used "spicy" language, and their conversations oftentimes dealt with their sex lives.

Thanks to these crusty women, I witnessed one of the funniest (and scariest) events I've ever seen, and I'm just thankful it didn't happen to me. A straight-out-of-college newbie was visiting the shop, learning how we did business on the Paveway line, and he stopped at a work station to ask a question. He was across from one of our loud and crusty assemblers, who was working while talking about her weekend exploits. She was a large woman, wearing a low-cut blouse which exposed an enormous cleavage. He was admiring the view when she looked up and caught him, and, without missing a beat, she said, "Well, honey, if you really want to see it, here you go." With that, she reached inside her bra, scooped out a large breast, and plopped it on the table. It lay there like a beached whale, as the laughter began. The newbie instantly turned bright red and began stammering, but he couldn't take his eyes off the breast, as it lay there on the table, mocking him. He backpedaled as fast as possible, until he backed into a work table; then he ran. The laughter echoed all over the shop, and catcalls followed him as other women piled on. As the newbie tried to escape, he bumped into another table and almost fell onto another woman, mainly because his eyes were still locked on that breast. The laughing turned into howling, and the woman calmly tucked her breast back into her blouse, stood up, and in a very loud voice, invited the newbie to join her after work for a "little sample." He ran away from the production area and was never seen again. He likely quit that same day out of sheer humiliation.

Of course, today that would be sexual harassment. As a leader, you will run into difficult situations that violate your standards. You have to be able to manage the behavior of a co-worker without showing the embarrassment which seems to egg others on. At the end of the day, a calm demeanor, and a dry retort ("As impressive as that is, do you really think it's appropriate?") can resolve a situation while minimizing damage.

Bull-Frogged

When I joined Texas Instruments, the Division Manufacturing Manager (I'll call him George) had been a successful manager for thirty years before I came on the scene.

> Don't be a "bull-frogger."

He was two levels above me, the epitome of the take-no-prisoners mentality, and he delighted in needling others. He viewed his role as one that included weeding out weak employees, and if you showed vulnerability, he attacked. Push back, and George respected you, but tuck your tail and slink away, and he would hound you until you quit. George enjoyed poking at people until they got angry, intentionally pushing them over the edge with a disparaging or insulting remark. When the target had more than he could stand and lashed out angrily, George would laugh and toss a printed business card across the table at the victim. The card had a picture of an angry bull frog, swollen and ready to explode. Across the bottom of the card was the inscription, "Congratulations, you've just been bull-frogged by George Banks." He thought it was hilarious, but recipients generally didn't agree. George was legendary for his political skills and the fear his bulldozer personality engendered in other employees.

"Bull-frogging" wasn't a trait I wanted in my management style. It was demeaning and often destructive. Even if the business culture around you supports bullying, you can choose not to make that *your* personal culture. Instead of following the herd, you should get your facts in order, argue data without emotion, and be willing to stand your ground, or you won't be respected. When disagreeing with someone else's position, never attack them personally or intentionally aggravate them. It always comes back to haunt you, and sometimes it results in escalating the disagreement and creating a problem that you lose control of. Instead, argue the data-specific reason to come around to your position. And when you've stood your ground for good reasons, be prepared for the other person to go over your head. Use data, and you'll always be all right … you may not win, but you'll have solid grounds for your position.

The Long Fall

In the 1980s, TI's Lewisville Security Director (let's call him Barney) came to TI after retiring from the military. He was a fifty-year-old pompous know-it-all who enjoyed wielding his authority. I was Site Manager, and although he reported to me on a dotted-line basis, Barney made it clear that he took his direction from TI's V.P. of Security. No one liked Barney, not even his staff (except for one person we'll discuss later). Barney directed an aggressive traffic patrol, running radar on site roads and patrolling parking lots for violators whose car tires touched one of the lines.

A group of important government visitors was traveling to the Lewisville site by helicopter, and Barney assigned his "crack combat troops" to establish a defensive perimeter around the helicopter landing site, just in case of terrorist attack. "Crack combat troops" is in quotes because the typical security officer was fifty or sixty years old, weighed at least fifty pounds more than his belt could accommodate, and wore a gun that rarely had bullets in it. To make the helicopter situation more humorous (scary?), each of Barney's troops was armed with either a riot gun or a semi-automatic assault weapon, along with a pistol. I was on the helicopter as it flew to the site with the dignitaries, and I saw the landing site from the air. The troops were smartly dressed in neatly pressed, new uniforms, and dark reflective sunglasses. All were prominently brandishing their weapons, facing outward for the slightest hint of enemy activity.

Barney was standing in the center of the circle, next to the helicopter pad, wearing mirrored sunglasses and barking orders to his troops. When we landed, neither Barney nor his troops looked inward, never made eye contact, and were on alert the whole time.

Barney had an assistant I'll call Barnette, second in command of security at the Lewisville site of 5,000 employees. Barnette was an attractive thirty-ish redhead, and her demeanor was similar to Barney's, drawing her importance from being second-in-command

> **Even the high and mighty can be brought low.**

to Barney. One sunny spring day at noon, one of Barney's crack troops was making his rounds in the parking lots, actually awake on this day, when he saw a van exhibiting suspicious behavior. Its engine was running, and it was rockin' and rollin', so he marched up to the van, intent on getting to the bottom of this nefarious business. He knocked on the sliding door, and the van came to a sudden halt in mid-roll, with no response. The crack troop was not to be dissuaded, and continued knocking until the side door slid slightly open. To his amazement, he saw Barney looking out, and behind him, scrambling to cover up with Barney's pants, was Barnette. Barney ordered the cop to depart, but called him to his office later in the day, attempting to force him to cover up the whole thing. To his credit, the security cop took his job seriously, and reported the incident up the chain. There was joy on the day Barney's employment was terminated, and Barnette was transferred to another site. The tersely-worded memo mentioned nothing of the cause for Barney's and Barnette's exit, but the rumor mill got it right, and the whole site had fun at their expense. Ah, how the great can fall. I interviewed Barney's successor, and he came into the job with a lot more humility.

Smoke 'Em If You Got 'Em

In the mid-1980s, Texas Instruments hired Nick Davis, a retired U.S. Army Colonel, as V.P. of Business Development. Nick had lost a leg to cancer, so he worked from a wheelchair, but he also liked to smoke cigars. TI's smoking policy required smokers to go to designated smoking areas within the facility to light up. For Nick, this wasn't a good solution, since he would have to roll his wheelchair more than 100 yards from his office to a DSA. My boss, Dean Clubb, made a controversial decision and directed me to carry it out, even though I didn't agree. He told me to establish a DSA close to Nick's office, so he could wheel out and smoke his cigars. After my protest, I acquiesced and we dropped an exhaust duct three feet above floor level on a window aisle outside Nick's office. Several times a day, he wheeled to his DSA and lit up. He sat with the cigar within one foot of the exhaust duct and blew smoke into the duct to keep it from drifting into the administrative area. Once in position, he held court with anyone who walked within shouting distance. I often found him there in his wheelchair, puffing away, with a group of people standing around him. It wasn't a pretty picture, nor did it meet the intent of TI's smoking policy, but it was a done deal.

We received complaints from employees who said they could smell the smoke, but the boss told us to ignore them. My contribution to this situation was the establishment of the "Stewart Standard for Exhaust Systems." I told our facility designer that the exhaust specification was simple: it had to "suck the hair off a tennis ball." This became a standard at our facility, and I took it with me when I left TI.

There are times when you're told to do something you don't agree with. You have four choices: comply, appeal, decline, or disregard the order. The first is often the right answer, but on occasions I've appealed an order, giving a good argument for reversing it, and was successful in reversing the decision. The third option, declining to implement the order, demands you have a very good reason. But it also requires you to meet with the boss to explain. Often, the boss will go elsewhere to accomplish the order, or perhaps rescind it. I've never been a fan of option four. I feel that disregarding your boss's direction is dishonest, and you owe it to him/her to deal with the issue directly.

The above also applies in the reverse direction. I've always encouraged my folks to push back if they didn't agree with something I asked them to do. I didn't commit to reverse direction, but I was always ready to give them an honest audience and listen to their arguments. At the end of the meeting, I made a decision, and the two of us agreed on a course of action. When they left my office, whether or not they changed my mind, they always left knowing they'd had a fair hearing, and there were never any repercussions for their disagreement.

> There are times when you're told to do something you don't agree with. You have four choices: comply, appeal, decline, or disregard the order.

You Had What Mailed to You at Work?

I received a call from TI's Lewisville Incoming/Receiving Supervisor one day, with a cryptic, "Uh, Mr. Stewart, I think you need to come see this." When I got there, in the middle of the room was a table with an open box on it. Around the table were eight people, looking down into the box, none of them touching it. I walked to the table and asked, "What's up?" The group parted soundlessly, allowing me to walk straight to the table, where the supervisor pointed to the box. When I looked into it, I understood why no one was getting close. The box was full of some of the craziest pornographic materials and sex toys imaginable! There were items in that box for which I could only suspect the use. So far, no one else had spoken a word, and they all looked up at the same time for my reaction. I sent everyone back to work, and the supervisor and I took the box to his office. He showed me the shipping label, which was addressed to an individual I knew, whom we'll call George.

George was a forty-five-year-old engineer working on a highly classified project, with a top secret security clearance … and apparently a few fetishes. If this type of information got out, it could be used to blackmail him, and the government took incidents of that sort very seriously. We called George to come to Receiving immediately.

George walked into the office where he saw the box, and I thought he was going to pass out on the spot. He had purchased pornography and "implements," and *used his real name!* Even worse, he had the order delivered to his work address, not realizing that every box that came to the plant was opened and inspected. George was mortified. I didn't have to ask whether the shipment was

> Dealing with human nature issues of this sort can be embarrassing, but they must be addressed honestly, directly, and in a timely manner.

his, and the only thing he said, over and over, was, "Please, don't tell my wife." George was almost catatonic for a while, and we had him sit down until he calmed down. He was so embarrassed, he would have run away if he thought it would keep his wife from finding out.

After a while, I took George to my office and called his manager, HR, and Security to join us. He was prepared to accept whatever decision was made, remorseful and awaiting his fate. In the end, we all agreed that we had to take disciplinary action, but it wouldn't necessitate termination of his employment. We made all the necessary disclosures, and George was put on probation for six months, which he served flawlessly. We never had an ounce of trouble from him again. And, no, we didn't tell his wife.

In any employee population of size, you can expect that the problems of society are also present. People are complex, and they're not always as rational as you might expect.

When You Assume. . .

In the mid-1980s, Texas Instruments was visited by a Congressional Staffer from the U. S. House Defense Committee, whom I'll call Susan. She had a Ph.D. from a prestigious university, and had recently transferred to the Defense Committee from another House committee. Susan held the senior staff position on a very important committee, responsible for writing Defense legislation and providing expert advice to committee members. She came to TI to learn about our technologies and products, so we took her visit very seriously. The briefing was classified secret, and we went all-out to give her a great introduction to TI. We spent the entire morning providing briefings by senior technologists, operations leaders, and product specialists, discussing our R&D breakthroughs for future weapon systems that the rest of the world only dreamed about. She sat through the entire meeting, nodding wisely, furrowing her brow, but asking few questions. We assumed she was on top of this thing, understanding what we were telling her, and absorbing the futuristic opportunities in the defense world. We put on a full-court press and felt good that we were blowing her away with our amazing technology (it *was* amazing, by the way). The day was going well, and after lunch it was time to take a tour.

I conducted the tour, and in one of our huge anechoic test chambers we paused to discuss the RF and noise-canceling capabilities of the chamber. I mentioned that with the doors closed, once our ears adjusted, we could even hear our hearts beat. When it was time to move on, Susan delayed the tour so she could listen to her heart beat. I suppose I should have gotten a clue at that moment.

After leaving the test facility, we walked to the main aisle of the Lewisville facility, which was a quarter of a mile long. I was discussing manufacturing technology when we were approached by an automated mail cart, which followed a reflective stripe painted on the floor. It toured the building, stopping at mail stations to allow people to pick up and drop off mail headed for other parts of the site. It was very basic, four feet tall, two feet wide, and four feet long, and we called it "Blue Eyes" for its two flashing blue warning lights on the front. It had a warning beeper that announced its presence, and it was interesting, but its technology was at least ten years old. Yawn, right?

As the cart approached, Susan was curiously observing it, so I stopped it and she inspected it from top to bottom. She asked questions, and I explained the automated vehicle, its reflective stripe, the programmed pick-up and delivery of mail, and the simple software that managed its travels. I was behind schedule, so I restarted the cart and moved on down the hall. But Susan kept hanging

> You will be most effective when you're able to assess others' capabilities and motivations, and communicate with them effectively on their level.

back, watching the departing cart. I couldn't believe it when this brilliant, powerful, political doctor-of-whatever, turned and asked, "Where is he?"

"Uh, where is who?" I asked.

Susan: "The driver."

Wayne: "Uh, what driver?"

Susan: "Where is the little guy who's driving the mail cart?"

I carefully explained again the automation and software, and she seemed to get it, so we continued our tour. However, at the end of the day she told us the highlight of her visit *was the stupid mail cart.*

Never assume that just because someone has a fancy degree, impressive resume, or powerful job that they have the same expertise, training, or knowledge-base you do. Start with the basics until you confirm the person's expertise level.

Charlie Wilson

Charlie Wilson, the Congressman from East Texas who visited Texas Instruments several times in the 1980s, was an American original. He was the subject of a "60 Minutes" story, the film "Charlie Wilson's War" starring Tom Hanks, and The History Channel's "The Real Story of Charlie Wilson." I got to know Charlie well, and from what I saw in those pieces, they were accurate depictions of Charlie's life. He is largely credited with defeating the Russians in Afghanistan in the 1980s, and his oversight of the intelligence community was fascinating. He always dressed immaculately in a fully-buttoned three-piece suit, white shirt, and perfectly knotted tie, sitting in the conference room ramrod stiff, sweating profusely, and in obvious distress. His hangovers were legendary, but he fought through the meetings, doing his job as a Congressman. He was a good TI friend, consistently supporting our products and recommending us to his congressional peers. Charlie was on the House Defense and Intelligence Committees, although his district had no defense facilities.

On one visit to TI, Charlie suggested we move Defense work to his East Texas district, in essence suggesting a *quid pro quo* in exchange for his support of our weapon systems in Congress. Charlie told us he was planning an East Texas "Supplier Day," where we could see the industrial capabilities of his district. I represented TI in a difficult situation, between a powerful Congressman who wanted to move work to his district, and Department of Defense acquisition rules.

I drove to Lufkin and met Charlie, his staff, and other industry representatives at his district office. He welcomed us and sent his staff with us on a tour of local companies, while he went to meetings with constituents and supporters, most likely at a local watering hole. We loaded onto Charlie's campaign bus and toured his district, going from company to company, meeting business owners, and discussing their potential to become defense suppliers. There were eight defense contractors on the tour, and we spent a very long day that concluded at Charlie's house that evening for cocktails and dinner.

Charlie was a bachelor, and his house was "1,000 percent a guy's place." The walls of his den and living room were covered with military memorabilia, including AK47s and other weapons. A framed display of military medals and battle ribbons caught my eye, and I realized I couldn't read the inscriptions, since they were in Cyrillic. Charlie walked over with a drink in his hand, and I asked him about the battle ribbons. He smiled and indicated he received them on one of his trips to Afghanistan, when his Mujahidin friends presented them to him as a token of their appreciation for supplying them with Stinger missiles that shot down Russian helicopters. Those battle ribbons and medals came from the uniform of the first Russian general killed in Afghanistan, shot down by a Stinger provided by Charlie.

Charlie was also a weapons collector. He led me to his bedroom, where he opened a special drawer that was filled with exotic and crazy military weapons. He took an Uzi to his bedroom balcony, and showed me how it worked … blasting a full magazine into the woods behind his house. When I gave him a "raised-eyebrow" query about the gunfire, he told me his old buddy, Sheriff Jim Bob, knew Charlie was harmless, and they'd laugh about it at the bar the next day.

> Sometimes winning isn't the other person's only objective.

I couldn't justify moving any purchases to Charlie's district, and was prepared for a call pressuring me to move business there, but it never came. I suppose Charlie just wanted to be able to tell his constituents that he tried.

Saudi Prince

I did not personally witness what I'm about to relate, but it's instructive, so I'm including it here. During production of the Paveway I FMS project, one of our customers came for a visit. Saudi Arabia was a long-time customer of TI's Geophysical Exploration business, using TI seismic-mapping technology in their oil business, and they were scheduled to receive some of the Laser Guided Bomb systems being produced on our contract. The Saudi team was headed by a prince, and the visit was intended to emphasize the importance of the relationship between the Saudi Kingdom and TI. A working lunch was scheduled with top TI executives at Dallas Headquarters, and some Einstein ordered a large sandwich tray from a local caterer. It was lovely, except that some of the sandwiches were ham. Since the Muslim faith forbids pork, the situation had the potential to be an international insult. One of the Prince's entourage saw a ham sandwich, and pointed to it, saying with outrage,

> When the stakes are high and someone on your team is potentially causing a major gaffe, as leader of the team it's up to you to resolve the situation before it goes critical. Humor can help bridge the gap to a new subject without losing face.

"Is that pork?" The room went deathly quiet as everyone realized how bad it could become.

The Prince, who had been educated in the U.S., calmly looked at the sandwich, picked it up and took a bite. He chewed reflectively, and said, "No, it is turkey."

The rest of the entourage relaxed. The Prince said it was turkey, so it had to be turkey. But I don't think any of them ate any of the sandwiches.

A Bad Performance Evaluation

Early in my career, I gave a performance review to a lady who had attendance and performance problems. She wasn't meeting work expectations, and I gave her a poor rating. Unfortunately, I violated a very important rule of performance evaluations: never surprise someone with a bad rating. Always provide feedback throughout the performance period, giving the employee a chance to improve.

We were sitting across a work table in a private area when I delivered the news. The woman became upset, crying and accusing me of being unfair. Her poor performance had been clearly documented, so I wasn't being unfair, but she obviously was not prepared to deal with a poor review. When she realized I wasn't going to change her rating, she quit crying, picked up her purse, and set it on the table. When she opened it, I saw a pistol inside. She looked at the gun, trying to decide what to do, and when she looked up, our eyes locked across the table. She saw me watching her, shut her purse, jumped up, and ran away. I called Security, and although she got out of the building before she could be intercepted, she was terminated immediately for bringing a gun on TI premises.

The woman made a wise choice to turn back from her anger before she did something that would have devastated both of our lives. I made a vow never again to surprise someone with a poor evaluation. From that point on, no matter how uncomfortable the discussions were, I resolved to give

> *Never* surprise someone with a poor performance evaluation.

timely and transparent performance feedback. Your people will appreciate the honest feedback, and if there are problems, be as specific as possible in defining a corrective action plan.

People Do What You Inspect, Not What You Expect

I don't believe the above is always true, but without question, there are people who are along for the ride. Uncommitted and disengaged, they can become a cancer on your organization and need to be weeded out so their poor attitudes don't infect others.

Defense Department (DoD) employees were assigned to our plant to provide "oversight" of our operations. Most were good folks, doing the job they were paid to do and committed to success. But there were some who weren't invested in their jobs or in achieving success. An example was a DoD inspector monitoring TI's missile systems production. He had a desk on a glass wall alongside a major hallway that I passed often. He arrived daily at 7:00 a.m. (and not one minute before) to an empty desk, set his thermos and newspaper on the desk, and went to the bathroom. Half an hour later, he returned to the desk, poured a cup of coffee, and began reading the newspaper. He spread it flat on the desk and read every word over the course of the day. At 8:30, he walked to a production area, where he wandered around for a few minutes, monitored the workers, and inspected products. He then went to another production area or returned to his desk, depending on how much time he'd been away at that point. Back at his desk, he poured more coffee and read more newspaper. At 11:00, he went to lunch. He normally made it back to the desk about 12:00.

His afternoon schedule was a repeat of the morning. At 2:55 p.m., he packed everything up and was out the door by 3:00 p.m. He worked the equivalent of three hours per day, but was paid for eight. In those days, his pay and benefits were likely higher than ours, and his attitude was horrible. He re-

> Some people aren't invested in their jobs or in achieving success.

sented having to work at all, and clearly disliked TI intensely, going out of his way to give us grief, just because he could. He answered to no one on site, and had likely been assigned to the job to get him out of the way. Rather than deal with performance problems or surplus personnel, they were shuffled around until they arrived somewhere "out of sight, out of mind." I've always been deeply resentful of those who collect a paycheck and don't give a second thought to being slackers.

Most people want to do a good job, and they enjoy being a part of a successful team. But there's a difference between people who are compliant versus those who are committed, and the productivity gap between them can be enormous. When you find employees who aren't engaged and committed, take action to either fix or fire them. Be sure you deal with the problem, though, and don't be perceived as shuffling a bad employee to someone else. Poor attitudes and lack of commitment will taint your organization, and you'll be tainted, too.

Transport Intercept

In the 1980s, one of Texas Instruments' black-world projects was under a schedule crunch and needed to deliver an item to a classified location across the country. This was one of those projects where no one was allowed to know the product, the project, the customer name, the destination, or anything else. Although the manufacturing organization reported to me, I was not briefed on the project, and to this day I don't know what it was. The product finished its testing on a Saturday, and it absolutely had to be delivered to the customer site by Monday. It was a long drive, and the delivery team had to leave that afternoon. There were stringent requirements for delivery, including three identical, unmarked and enclosed vans, with two employees per vehicle, radio clearance, and "no stop" orders. TI vehicles were not available that Saturday afternoon, so my Operations Manager went to a local car dealership and bought three vans on his company credit card.

I had to be available all day to confirm the authenticity of the order and clear the amount through American Express. The amount wasn't the issue, but getting the registrations and titles, and clearing the dealership hurdles was a feat.

The vans loaded and began driving north into Oklahoma. The middle van had the product, and the other vans were in front and behind. They weren't allowed to stop, except to refuel, for the entire trip, and they were not to raise any suspicions whatsoever. Under no conditions were they allowed to open the van doors, nor were they allowed to carry any weapons.

Somewhere in Oklahoma a state trooper became suspicious for some reason, although the vehicles were not speeding, as they were under strict orders to remain unobtrusive. But of course, they had to obey law enforcement. Quite a dilemma.

Smokie pulled behind the vans and turned on his lights. The vans pulled over, and when the officer approached, he demanded that the drivers open the vans. The TI drivers politely refused, and they took no action except to park, step out of the vehicles, and provide their drivers licenses. Outnumbered and suspicious, Smokie became surly and again demanded the vans be opened, warning he would arrest the employees if they didn't comply. I'm sure Smokie had visions of a huge pile of illegal drugs and drug kingpins, and becoming a hero in the community. But the TI employees couldn't allow the van to be opened, and they wouldn't identify themselves, other than to provide their drivers licenses. When Smokie continued to demand access to the vans and information of all sorts he wasn't cleared to have, the only answer he got was, "You are not authorized to receive that information."

Smokie was really angry by now. He drew his weapon and put the employees against the side of the van to arrest them all. They told him he could not arrest them, nor could he delay them any longer, which poured gasoline on a Smokie fire. He called for back-up and became really angry and aggressive.

> What looks like a "slam dunk" deal may not turn out that way.

The saving point was "the number," supplied with the travel orders. It put the caller in immediate contact with someone in the government who had lots of authority. The message was, "You are not allowed to open or see inside this van, and you need to call this number to confirm our orders." This was before cell phones, so when the TI employee gave Smokie the number and told him to call it, he grudgingly radioed headquarters, and his commanding officer made a call to "the number."

When the Sergeant made the call and realized who he was talking to, he was told in no uncertain terms to get that trooper the hell out of the way of that vehicle. The Sergeant called Smokie back, and whatever he said, Smokie came to attention, turned a deep red color, and said, "Yes sir," multiple times. He returned to the vans with his figurative hat in his hands, apologized, and offered to escort the vans to the Kansas border at high speed. Our guys said, "No, thank you," and drove off on their mission.

When We Lose Employees

From time to time, my job at Texas Instruments required me to deal with the deaths of employees. Two instances come to mind. The first involved one of our technicians who attended an off-site, after-hours party with a number of TI employees and spouses. Late in the evening, he got drunk and began trying to get close to the wife of another employee. The husband was also under the influence, and despite several requests, the first employee continued to misbehave. Most people at this point would have left the party, dragging his wife with him, but the husband decided he'd had enough. He went to his truck, returned with a shotgun, and shot the offending employee in the face, killing him. Since the death occurred away from work, I wasn't directly involved in dealing with the situation, although we provided support to the families for some time. Both employees had been good performers with no history of bad blood or aggressive behavior, and there was never an adequate explanation for a tragedy that destroyed several people's lives that night.

The second situation involved an employee I'll call Jim. He was fifty years old, and worked a couple of levels down in my organization. Jim was driving home late one night on a freeway when he spotted a disabled car and a young lady on the shoulder waving at passing cars for help. When Jim stepped out of his car to lend assistance, the girl's boyfriend stepped out from the shadows and shot Jim in the stomach. The two robbed him and stole his car. A passer-by called 911, and Jim got to the hospital in time to be saved. He underwent months of rehabilitation and finally was cleared to come back to work.

We moved Jim to a job that accommodated his recovery, and he and I became friends. He dropped by my office every so often, and we talked about his health, work, and family. Jim had been a heavy smoker and drinker, and though he stopped during his recovery, after several months he resumed his bad habits. A year later, Jim had a heart attack, and he underwent quadruple bypass surgery, from which he had a hard time recovering. He spent an extended time in a coma, and when he regained consciousness, his pain levels were high. He became addicted to powerful pain pills, and though he was eventually released from the hospital, his health was precarious. We kept Jim on our employee rolls on disability status the entire time so he could retain medical benefits.

After his doctors released him for limited work, Jim came to TI to discuss his return, and I met with him. He was frail, and doctors gave him stringent restrictions. He had again sworn off cigarettes and alcohol and seemed to be in a positive frame of mind. We arranged for Jim to work at a desk job, starting with half-days until his recovery allowed him to return to full days. Everything was going well until he visited his doctor a few months later and received a bad report. I don't know what his doctor told him, but Jim called to ask for a meeting. I was literally walking out the door on my way to the airport, so I was only able to talk with him briefly on the phone. Though he sounded depressed, he didn't say anything alarming, and I asked him to wait until I returned from my business trip to get together. He agreed, and I hung up thinking we'd sort it all out then.

> No matter how good your managerial skills are, there will be tragedies that can profoundly affect you.

Evidently Jim's depression worsened over the weekend, he began drinking and smoking again, and his wife couldn't get him to stop. She told me later that all he wanted to do was sit in the backyard and drink and smoke. Sunday night, a few hours before he was to meet with me, Jim shot and killed himself in his backyard.

To the day I die, I will wonder what I might have done differently to help Jim see a different future. I was prepared to work with him to accommodate his restrictions and ensure his medical insurance remained in force. I undoubtedly failed Jim, although I don't know what I should have done differently. I suppose I could have cancelled my business trip and met with him immediately, but I didn't detect any suicidal warning signs. His wife didn't blame me; after all, I was only his employer, and I had no responsibility for what he did … right? … right? … RIGHT?

Another Bad Performance Review

In any large organization, there are employees who are along for the ride and attempt to take advantage of you and the company. Your obligation to the company puts you in a position of having to discern real versus marginal issues, and deliver bad news with firmness and humanity.

DEALING WITH BIG PERSONALITIES

A thirty-five-year-old woman I'll call Margaret was working as an engineer in Texas Instruments' Lewisville organization. She'd been a marginal performer over a three-year period and had gone out on two medical leaves of absence. When she was working, Margaret was rarely on time, her work quality was not good, and she did not always behave as a professional. Two months after returning from her most-recent medical leave, Margaret's supervisor counseled her on poor work performance, and she immediately claimed a work-related back injury, and produced a doctor to support her need for a third medical leave. Four months later, when Margaret was cleared to come back to work, it was time for her performance review and she received a bad rating. She reacted angrily and demanded a meeting with me to appeal her treatment.

When Margaret entered my office without a trace of a limp or discomfort, she was bright, cheerful, and energetic. She was an attractive woman, and flirting outrageously was a personality trait she used to get what she wanted. I got the impression she was skilled at it, and as I listened to Margaret's story, I was struck by her lack of acceptance of any responsibility for her situation. She attempted to steer me to her side without addressing her performance issues. When she perceived I wasn't going to succumb to her flirting, she shifted gears, complaining of another back injury she had not previously mentioned.

I stopped the discussion and asked Margaret if she felt she'd injured her back again. She went into her act, crying and slumping in her chair, followed by slowly tipping to the side and falling out of the chair onto the floor. I didn't move from behind my desk. I called my secretary into the office to provide a witness for what was to come next. I asked Margaret if she had injured her back previously, or while she was sitting in a chair at my desk, since she hadn't shown any signs of pain as she entered my office. She nodded and cried steadily, so I asked if I should call an ambulance, to which she shook her head and climbed back into her chair, still sniffling. Unemotionally, I said I found it curious that her back had only that instant begun to bother her, and that I felt she was abusing her situation. Further, I said her performance review was correct, and she needed to get back to work where she could begin improving her performance.

Margaret stood up huffily, told me she expected more from me than that, and stormed (painlessly) out of my office. I had my secretary document everything she saw, I did the same, and I instructed HR that the performance review would stand. I expected Margaret either to resign, or we would begin disciplinary action moving toward terminating her employment.

> Failure to act when confronted with employees taking advantage of policies makes you part of the problem.

Margaret resigned the next day, and we never heard from her again. Margaret's situation was flagrant abuse of the medical policy to escape accountability.

Giving Up Instead of Giving In

When I worked at Texas Instruments' Sherman, Texas plant, my secretary, Susan, had chronic back pain, and it impacted her performance and attendance. She had back surgery years earlier, but it hadn't corrected her problem and she tried to work through it. After months of pain, she found a doctor who prescribed a pain management process that looked like torture. She wore a battery pack with wires embedded in her back, and somehow this device ("Sparky") sensed her pain and sent an electrical shock into her back. I don't know how effective it was, but it created bizarre reactions. Every so often, Sparky discharged, and Susan jerked spasmodically and quivered a little until "Sparky" turned off the juice. It would have been comical if she hadn't been so miserable. She would be in mid-sentence and suddenly jerk upright, clench her jaw, and jiggle a little. When the power turned off, she would shake her head and carry on with the conversation.

Susan came to my office one day, complaining that her back wasn't allowing her to work, and that she had called her son to come get her.

She was almost frantic with pain and embarrassment, and told me she was going to resign. I offered to help her to the door, but she jumped up, grabbed her personal items from her desk and ran, vibrating every few steps, to the exit. Her son came to pick her up, and she went home. Susan resigned, which was a shame because she lost her medical insurance coverage. I would gladly have supported her with a leave of absence, but she never gave me the chance. I never heard from her again.

> As a manager, you have to be discerning, helping when appropriate, being strong when not, and representing the company's interests in dealing with issues.

Employees deserve our compassionate support when they encounter issues in their lives. Their health and families are their first priorities, and I've never found a situation where I couldn't help an employee with a legitimate problem.

Allen Thomas

Allen Thomas was the long-time program manager of the Harpoon program in Texas Instruments' Defense Business, and he was tapped in 1986 to move to Lewisville to take over program management for the HARM missile program. I was Division Operations Manager, responsible for manufacturing of HARM and a number of other classified programs. I had an excellent working relationship with the prior HARM program manager, handling forecasting and financial management for much of the program, in addition to my operations responsibilities. Allen, on the other hand, was an intense, controlling program manager with a notoriously short and raging temper. Nothing happened on his program without his approval, which represented a huge change from my relationship with the prior program manager. Allen and I bumped heads a number of times, especially when our President, Bill Mitchell, directed me to make changes in manufacturing that affected the HARM program. Allen's response was, essentially, "Go pound sand." If I had possessed the experience and demeanor I have now, I may have been able to finesse Allen to agree, but back then, when someone told me I couldn't do something, I responded by deciding I was going to do it. Over the years, we had a number of serious battles, and Allen won more than I did. Despite the battles, we respected one another, and though Allen was harsh at times, he was also extremely disciplined. He was at an age and tenure that demanded respect.

> Billy goats often get their way, but that isn't usually the best way to get what you want.

Allen had a number of colloquialisms that he brought out at appropriate times. When he disagreed with someone, rather than discussing the issue and trying to maintain a civil relationship, he was apt to say, "Go butt a stump," or, "Go pound sand," meaning, "This discussion is over, you lose, knock yourself out, but you're not messing with my program." If someone had a dilemma with an unclear path and risk on both sides of a decision, Allen would say, "Looks like you're between the dog and the fireplug." If someone did something he didn't like, he marched into the office, slammed the door, and said, "I've got a bone to pick with you, and I'm going to pick it clean." If he heard that someone outside his group was doing something he didn't like, he was apt to say, "Just kill him and tell God he died."

As humorous as Allen's sayings may have been, they were delivered in a way that made a strong point. People ignored his warnings at their peril; he could be a very disagreeable man. Allen died "in the saddle" while working at TI, suffering a heart attack that killed him a few days later. As much head-butting as we did, he was an outstanding program manager, and I respected him greatly.

Gristly Chicken

I learned more about brash, driven management from Bill Mitchell, President of Texas Instruments' Defense Business and E.V.P. of TI, than anyone in my career. He led the HARM Missile program through development and production phases to become the largest program in TI history,

> Know your bosses and their preferences. I'm just sayin' … .

surpassing Paveway for that honor. He liked to keep in touch with his employees, so he held periodic roundtable lunches with randomly selected employees. As Site Manager, I organized the luncheons when he came to Lewisville, Texas, where 5,000 of his employees worked, but the actual meal arrangements were handled by our cafeteria manager. On one occasion, grilled chicken was served, a dish he'd served before with good results, so he thought Bill would like it. Well, he didn't like it, saying it was "gristly." He complained to my boss, Dean Clubb, S.V.P. of the Defense Suppression Business, who called me to his office and demanded to know why the chicken was gristly.

Now, Dean was a rare individual, an inspiring leader, brilliant engineer, and excellent communicator. I learned more about communications and leadership from him than from anyone else. But in this case, I thought he was just flat wrong. I must have been in a bad mood, because the inquiry seemed to be a complete waste of my time, and my reply was something like, "How should I know that?"

That wasn't good enough, and he demanded that I do an investigation of the cafeteria operation and the chicken supplier to determine why the chicken was gristly and what we were going to do about it. My response was angry: "I can't believe you're seriously asking me to do an in-depth investigation and failure analysis of gristly chicken. I consider that a waste of time when we're working hard every day to improve the performance of our division." I had never refused one of his assignments before, and he backed off. We agreed that I should send the complaint to the cafeteria manager, and I never heard the words "gristly chicken" again.

My mentor, Jim Houlditch, thought it was funny, except that I was obviously so mad. He said, "You never should have served chicken to Bill. He doesn't like chicken."

"How the hell am I supposed to know that?" I asked.

Jim said, "You should have called his secretary to ask what he likes to eat."

When you're in charge of providing amenities for executives and dignitaries, it's well worth your time to make a few calls to learn their preferences, and, more importantly, what's off-limits. Whether or not it's the best use of your time, just do it!

Fire Drill Disaster

The Sherman Democrat was the Sherman, Texas local newspaper when I was at that Texas Instruments' plant, and let's just say there was no love lost between the Site Manager (we'll call him Jeff) and the newspaper. The paper had burned Jeff on several occasions with blindsides, misquotes, and negative stories, so there was

> You can't control your message all the time, but know that bad actors seldom change their ways.

mistrust in the relationship. He took a call one day from the newspaper's publisher, who wanted to try to improve damaged relations; after all, TI was the largest employer in the county. Jeff didn't trust the newspaper to give TI a fair shake, but when the publisher asked sincerely if there were any interesting upcoming TI events, Jeff mentioned an upcoming fire drill. That's pretty benign, right? How can a newspaper make something negative out of a fire drill?

So Jeff hosted the publisher and a photographer, and the group went up on the roof of the three-story main building to watch the drill. Right on time, the fire alarms went off, and TI employees began filing out of the doors on all sides of the building. The photographer took a number of pictures, and the publisher and Jeff talked about the successful fire drill. They shook hands and congratulated one another on a good start to improving relations.

But it's hard for a tiger to change his stripes. The next day, on the front page of *The Sherman Democrat*, was a large rooftop photograph of TI's employees exiting the building in a safe and orderly manner. The headline at the top of page one: "TI Employees Walk Out." The publisher of *The Sherman Democrat* thought it was funny. Jeff didn't.

"60 Minutes"

What follows was a painful lesson in modern media. Despite doing everything right, Texas Instruments was painted in the worst possible way by a politician and media with an agenda.

The altitude sensor was one of thousands of parts used in the HARM system, delivered from hundreds of suppliers around the country. Each part was governed by a specification that defined performance, quality, reliability, and testing requirements, and suppliers were required to test and certify compliance with the specification and supply test data for critical parts. Due to a whistleblower at the altitude sensor's facility, we discovered the supplier had falsified test data for a lot (production run) of parts. The issue was escalated to the upper echelons of the Navy and the FBI investigated the allegations. TI undertook an immediate investigation, confirming the supplier's fraud and reporting our findings to the Navy and FBI. By that time, some of the parts had already been delivered in HARM missiles, so we had both production and field problems.

John Dingell of Michigan was the longest-serving congressman in history, originally elected in 1955, and Chairman of the House Energy and Commerce Committee. Congressman Dingell heard about the issue and called for House Banking Committee hearings, despite having no jurisdiction in the matter.

Somewhere along the line, producers for the television program "60 Minutes" learned of the problem and decided to do a story. The producers contacted TI, and they were invited to Dallas for two days of meetings to discuss the issue. We went open-book with them, relaying how we discovered the

> Behave honorably and fix mistakes, and be wary of media with an agenda.

falsifications, providing documentation of our actions, and discussing our role in any story they might undertake. When Navy and FBI investigations completed, TI was exonerated, and we provided the producers with Navy and FBI letters confirming that TI had acted appropriately.

Mike Wallace, one of the most aggressive—and, many say, unfair—investigative journalists on television, was assigned the story. Based on Wallace's reputation as a hatchet man with an agenda, TI declined to participate in the story, and refused to allow "60 Minutes" to come on site. When Wallace and his film crew showed up at the Lewisville facility, cameras rolling, they were stopped at the lobby, and as site manager, I got to assist Mr. Wallace and his crew in finding the exit. The next day, they hired a helicopter and circled the TI site, filming. They set up a camera and stood at the front gate attempting to interview employees as they entered and left the facility, but no one spoke with them.

When it aired, the "60 Minutes" story implied that TI was complicit in the fraud. There was no mention of the Navy and FBI investigations exonerating TI. Interviews of Navy and FBI officials were edited in such a way that any positive comments about TI did not appear. The supplier's CEO was interviewed *in prison*, and he had nothing negative to say about TI.

Congressman Dingell was filmed as part of the story, and when Mike Wallace asked his opinion of TI's role in the fraud, Dingell said something along the lines of, "At best, gross incompetence; at worst, they were part of the fraud." As the helicopter flew above the TI Lewisville site, Wallace said that Texas Instruments officials declined to be interviewed on camera. He didn't mention that TI officials had discovered and disclosed the problem and had spent two days providing open-book access to his producers. He didn't mention that, despite not being responsible, TI offered to replace all altitude sensors free to the Navy.

Bill Mitchell, President of the Defense Group, was apoplectic and demanded that TI unleash its lawyers in lawsuits against "60 Minutes." But TI's executive team decided to let everything settle. After things quieted, there were no repercussions from the government, and the negative publicity died quickly.

When Employees Betray You

Ethics are invaluable, and my own and my groups' integrity was non-negotiable. This goes to the heart of credibility, which is critical to any organization; you must say what you do, and do what you say. Unfortunately, no matter how much you emphasize integrity, there will be times when people betray you with unethical decisions or actions. On such occasions, no matter how valuable the person is, you must take action, or his/her action will become yours. If you don't come down strongly on the side of integrity, you risk being painted with the same brush (of suspicion and condemnation) as the person who betrayed you. Over my career, I'm sad to say I had to deal with too many unethical behaviors. These were all real situations.

- An employee who took kickbacks from a supplier
- A peer who set up a dummy corporation for fraudulent purchasing
- A boss who blamed his people in public for things he did
- An employee who went to jail for illegal purchasing actions
- A competitor who asked me to share bid pricing information
- Drug trafficking on-site
- A supplier who let it be known that a non-professional relationship might be in order

- Employees who propositioned and groped other workers
- A supplier who falsified product test data
- An employee who defrauded an insurance company
- A peer who asked me to falsify a test report
- An employee who falsified expense reports
- A customer who negotiated in bad faith; covering up substantial errors
- Employees who carried on affairs *on company premises*
- An employee who killed another employee.

As painful as it may have been, doing the right thing was always the correct course of action. In some cases, that meant an employee lost his job, or went to jail. Making exceptions for favorites can get you in trouble, and my process for dealing with problems was to perform a review of the situation,

> The integrity of an organization begins (and ends) at the top.

in some cases calling in third parties on occasion to ensure thorough investigations. It was my responsibility to understand the situation and make a documented decision for action. There was never any confusion which side of the issue I came down on. As a rule of thumb, I applied the "newspaper criteria" to a critical decision, "How would my decision look, if it appeared on the front page of *The Dallas Morning News* with my name attached to it?"

Over my forty year professional career, I and my organizations were never sued or taken to court. I've never been called to testify in a court case, and, except for a few bad apples I dealt with for committing illegal acts, I'm happy to report that my organizations have modeled high levels of ethics and integrity.

You must clearly define for your organization your ethical expectations, then hold yourself and your organization accountable. Don't be the person who embarrasses the company. Be transparent when investigating problems, and ensure you hear both sides of every problem, because *there are always two sides*. Bring in Human Resources, Security, Purchasing, etc. as appropriate and obtain their advice before making a decision. And when you communicate your decision, be sure you look your employee in the eye when you unequivocally define the problem and the outcome.

Jana and the Memory Stick

What follows was hilarious, although it could be considered sexist. Some employees could have been offended, but my friend Jana is such an outstanding leader, she made it all OK. With apologies to my good friend, the story is just too good not to include.

Jana Gerber was a wonderful friend and Schneider Electric business associate. At the time of this story, she was SE's Americas Marketing Director. Jana was eight months pregnant and had recently scored a huge marketing success in New York City. She put on a security expo which included Tom Ridge, former Director of Homeland Security, as the keynote speaker. It had been a great success, and Jana was receiving kudos all around for her excellent work organizing and executing the event.

The New York event was to be followed a day later by a stock analysists meeting back in Dallas, and Jana, jet-lagged and tired, was to moderate the meeting. At the early morning dry-run for the meeting later that day, Jana loaded her presentation onto the computer, and the screen over her head flashed into life. Head down, she was busy working on something else. What she did not know was that while in New York, her computer had somehow picked up a virus. It had infected the memory stick on which her presentation files resided.

Raucous laughter broke out, and Jana finally looked up to see what was so funny. There, up on the screen was the most lurid pornography imaginable. When she saw the porn, she turned beet red and began struggling to minimize the damage. Warren Rosebraugh, who was closest to Jana, reached over and pulled the memory stick from the computer. She began trying to explain how pornography got onto her computer, but no one was buying it. She took some loud, good-natured hootin' and hol-lerin' before things settled down. But Jana plowed ahead and delivered a highly-successful analysts meeting.

Several days later, the entire executive team assembled for the staff meeting: the Board Room was full of V.P.s and Directors, and the speaker phone was filled with additional staff members. Initial conversations were winding down, and an expectant hush swept the room, when someone mentioned Jana's

> Be willing to laugh at yourself, and don't ever take yourself too seriously.

porn episode. The executives demanded to hear the whole story. So Jana, with good-natured assistance from several of the executives, recounted the porn saga, and there was a lot more hootin' and hollerin', which Jana took with good humor. She let everyone, especially the boss, know the porn was caught and removed before there was any damage.

The laughter and commentary continued, as the executive team en-joyed the mental image of eight-months-pregnant Jana, with a porn-infected laptop, scrambling to correct the embarrassing situation.

Jana, trying to extricate herself, said something that will live forever: "The porn was on the stick, but Warren pulled it out before there was any damage."

I have no idea where this came from, but in the next few seconds of silence, I looked down at Jana's tummy and said, "Apparently not soon enough."

The entire room collapsed, roaring with laughter. The speaker phone added its raucous noise, and Jana kept trying to explain, without success. It was undoubtedly the funniest work event in my career, with executives overcome with laughter, and the president literally fell out of his chair. People on the conference phone were laughing uncontrollably, and the volume in the room was well over 100 decibels.

Jana's face was red as she tried to explain. Everything she said elicited more gales of laughter. Finally, she gave in and joined the merriment. By the time it was over, the event had entered the annals of legendary gaffs.

Dealing with Big Personalities

All of us can learn from her misfortune. She violated one of the indelible rules of holes: "When trying to climb out of a hole you've dug for yourself, the first rule is to stop digging."

Chapter Seven

Negotiating as an Artform

L ife is full of negotiations, both professional and personal. Many of your daily interactions are negotiations that you don't even notice. Dealing successfully with others is dependent on recognizing and effectively managing expectations—both your own and theirs'. The art/science of negotiating and adopting effective techniques for improving outcomes are of great benefit.

Early in my career, I had the opportunity to take a negotiations training course, "Effective Negotiations," by Chester A. Karrass. It was the most beneficial training of my entire career, dealing with expectation management, negotiation strategy and tactics, and optimizing negotiation outcomes. The techniques I learned have served me well in hundreds of negotiations over the years in domestic, government, international, commercial, and charitable settings.

Paveway I Learning Ground

Texas Instruments began production of Paveway I systems, in Sherman, Texas, in 1978, although contract negotiations hadn't yet completed. Unlike many government contractors, TI preferred Firm Fixed-Price (FFP) contracts that provided the opportunity to aggressively execute projects, drive down costs, and generate additional profit by project end. The Foreign Military Sales (FMS) office within the Department of Defense (DoD) had authorized foreign sales of Paveway I systems for a number of countries, once the advanced Paveway II system went into production. We were being pressed to get production underway as soon as possible, but when negotiations weren't completed quickly, Paveway I production

> **Always take the higher road.**

began without a finalized contract. The program came into production efficiently, but with each passing day more cost history was being accumulated, and the FFP contract began to look more like a low-profit, cost-plus contract.

The Air Force FMS contracting office was at Hill Air Force Base in Ogden, Utah, and I was on the team negotiating the contract with DoD personnel. Working with military officers over the years was enjoyable, typically honorable, hard-working, mission-driven professionals. But some DoD civilians who performed audits, negotiated, and administered contracts could be a challenge.

After numerous scandals, DoD implemented a program called "Straight Arrow," requiring all government employees to pay their own way when dealing with contractors. They were not allowed to accept gifts, entertainment, or even normal business lunches. For lunch meetings with DoD personnel, we put a cash box on the table with a slot in the top where government folks could pay for their meals. Civilians never asked the cost of the meal, and they made a show of dropping money into the box. When I later emptied the boxes, I never found more than a few one dollar bills. Conversely, when military personnel were in attendance, they typically paid more than would have been expected.

During one particularly contentious negotiation, the DoD Contracting Officer and I thought it would be good for our teams to get together for drinks and appetizers at a local watering hole, to try to reduce stress a little. We had three rounds of drinks over two hours, and when the get-together broke up, as they left, the government folks pitched some cash on the table to pay for their share, then left. I was stuck with the bill, which was over $500 for eight people, five of whom were government employees. The amount of money they left on the table was $16.

Negotiation Ethics

Texas Instruments' cost proposal for the first Paveway I project in Sherman, Texas supported a price of more than $40 million. It was well substantiated with historical data, supplier quotes, analyses, and documentation. I had personally put the proposal together, and it was rock solid. Since this would be a Firm Fixed-Price (FFP) contract, all the risk fell on TI, and problems would be on TI to resolve or suffer the profit penalties. We expected to settle the contract somewhere in the $38 million range, and then we'd bust our butts to execute well and gain additional profit. We provided reams of audited historical data to the government team, and spent hours explaining in excruciating detail the rationale and mathematical foundation for our pricing. Government auditors supported more than ninety-five per cent of our price, so we felt confident we'd gain a fair settlement. Anticipating an initial offer from the government of about $35 million, we expected to settle somewhere between our $40 million and their $35 million. That's what negotiations are for.

Their initial offer was $18 million—a huge slap in the face! When I asked the Contracting Officer why, his response was, "Because I could. I know our auditors supported your price, but I don't care; I don't have to be reasonable."

Thus began eight months of rancorous negotiations at Hill AFB in Utah. We made sixteen trips there, leaving early on Mondays, and returning late on Fridays. They kicked our butts needlessly, and there's no telling how much money and time was wasted on both sides. We finished at $38 million, but they got their pound of flesh, and they enjoyed extracting it.

One DoD cost analyst was a man from Utah I'll call Barry, and he was a royal jerk. He was a tall, skinny man with an arrogant, condescending attitude, and an irritating smirk that could drive the Pope to drink. At one point during negotiations, he gave us an offer with an attached rationale that supposedly justified his offer. I detected a mistake in his calculations, which when corrected yielded a price much more in our favor. I called him on the error, and when he realized his mistake, he smirked, and said, "I withdraw the offer. Here's the new offer," and wrote the same number on a piece of paper, this time with no rationale, and shoved the paper at me. I confronted him for taking an unethical action, and

> Never surrender your own principals, and don't hesitate to call the other side when they attempt something unethical.

he just sneered and said, "I don't care, it's your turn to make an offer." I appealed to the Contracting Officer, who was now on the defensive, since he couldn't condone unethical behavior, and he came back with a better offer. Barry sat and grinned smugly; no skin off his bureaucratic backside.

On another occasion, I caught Barry in a blatant lie. He said something outrageous and untrue, and I called him on it. Caught red-handed, he (once again) smirked and said, "OK, rule 19."

"What's that?" I asked.

He said, "Per rule 19, a lie is not a lie when the truth is not expected to be spoken." Barry showed it to me in government training materials, which essentially gave government representatives authorization to behave in an unethical manner when they felt it would benefit them. Contractors behaving similarly could potentially be charged with criminal offenses. Barry thought it was humorous, saying, "I don't have to tell the truth or behave ethically because I'm the government, and you shouldn't expect truth from the government."

Negotiations Completed

Negotiations on the Texas Instruments' Paveway I FMS contract were protracted and contentious, though we finally achieved a reasonable price. Both sides got a black eye, and TI executives had to be called in to finish the deal. The entire bid, audit, and negotiation process had taken more than a year, and during that time we executed a significant portion of the contract, with the costs becoming "actuals." In the last negotiation session, with our Vice President in attendance, we sat across the table from the DoD team, and things went sour. It was good for our V.P. to see first-hand Barry's unreasonable arrogance, and his sneering, condescending demeanor was directed at our VP.

At one session, Barry presented an insulting counter-offer, with derisive and condescending commentary. It was hand-written on a sheet of paper and shoved disrespectfully across the table. We looked at it, and recognized the proposal was counter-productive. Our V.P. picked up the piece of paper, trying to control his anger, and said, "This is not appropriate. You owe us a reasonable offer." He lifted the paper and gave it a shove at chest level across the table. The paper sailed like a kid's airplane, gliding the full width of the table until it hit the contracting officer directly in the chest.

The man rose angrily to his feet, wadded up the paper and threw it back across the table, yelling, "Well, you don't have to throw it in my face." He stormed out of the conference room, followed by the rest of the government negotiation team. It was all for show, an interesting but unsuccessful tactic. After they slammed the door on the way out of the room, they could be heard laughing, and we burst out laughing as well.

After a respectable time passed, they came back in the room, never mentioned the outburst, and gave us another offer—a more reasonable one. We finished negotiations that week, after months of traveling to Utah, watching the mountains turn from frigid winter to lush summer foliage. After enduring months of hotel rooms and poor dinners, we finally got it done. After it was over, our V.P. commented that he didn't know how we'd put up with it for a year.

Once negotiations completed, we turned our attention to executing the remainder of the three-year contract, which yielded outstanding results. We implemented productivity improvements and were able to achieve a level of profitability above what had been projected.

I loved the role of Project Manager, leading a high-performance team, challenging for better performance, solving problems, and being part of a huge success. It was a rewarding time of my career. I could personally touch the products and the processes, know everyone involved, enjoy

> In some ways, negotiations are games. Everyone has expectations for the outcome, often contrary to others'.

the camaraderie of mutual objectives and shared successes, tackle problems and deliver solutions, and be recognized for my work. It doesn't get any better than that!

Finding common ground, helping the other side find a "win," and delivering solid solutions are mostly the product of good preparation, relentless determination, and ethical business practices.

The TI59 Calculator

Texas Instruments invented the calculator in the late 1960s, the first of which was a four-function model called the TI Datamath. In the second half of the 1970s, TI developed the first programmable calculator, the TI59. It was actually a hand-held computer, with a portable printer and magnetic memory cards. TI issued a TI59 to every professional employee as a productivity tool. I enjoyed working with mine, since it allowed me to use my programming skills in a directly-applicable way.

In the late 1970s, prior to beginning negotiations for the second Paveway I contract, I developed a pricing program that used DoD's cost elements and pricing structure It accommodated more than sixty variables and pricing factors, and generated a full-cost position in standard DoD format. I could run multiple "what ifs" and print out an offer for the government in just a few minutes.

Government negotiations usually included offer exchanges, often highly technical, with detailed lists of cost elements and calculations. Prior to the TI59, a manual offer could take several hours to prepare.

But with the TI59, I was able to automate the offer preparation process, plugging in cost factors and punching the "go button." The printout detailed the entire offer, and when handed to the government negotiators, it essentially said, "Here's our offer; the ball's in your court."

A common negotiation tactic was to position your offer at the end of the day. That way, the other side had to work late into the evening to prepare an offer for presentation the next morning. The first time I brought my TI59 to a negotiation session, I set it in the center of the table and plugged it in without explanation. The government team looked at it suspiciously, and Barry condescendingly threw out, "What's that supposed to be?"

I replied, "Oh, just a new tool we've developed to help us develop our positions."

Late that afternoon, the government presented an offer and began packing up, leaving us to work late. I asked for a minute before adjourning, punched several factors into my TI59, and ran a new offer. The government folks watched curiously, and when the printer started printing, they craned their necks to read what was spitting out. The printer finished, I tore off the offer sheet, and handed it to the government team. I explained how to read the printout, and since they'd never seen anything like it, they were absolutely dumbfounded. It was sooooo gratifying to see the incredulous looks on their faces. They stammered aimlessly as it sunk in that they'd now have to work late instead of us.

I said, "Gentlemen, here is our offer with all the details. We'll adjourn and see you in the morning when you can provide us with your counter-offer." We stood up and left, with the government side still sitting at the table, all four of them gathered around our offer sheet as it lay on the table. No one would touch it, as though it was radioactive, but they realized something had fundamentally changed in their world. Our team had a great evening, reliving the highlight of our trip.

The TI59 program could also reproduce the government's position, essentially checking their math. On several occasions, I found errors in their offers, pointed them out, and asked that they be corrected. A couple of times they agreed, but mostly they blustered about relevance and left their offer on the table. On one occasion, I found an error in our favor, and I demonstrated good faith by pointing it out to them. That made an impression, and from then on, the tone of our negotiations elevated, with trust and ethics becoming the norm. If

> Sometimes a change introduced into a negotiation can provide you with unexpected advantage.

they failed to correct an error in their favor, we made an allowance for their error in our next offer, staying one step ahead of them. They were constantly on the defensive and didn't like it a bit.

The TI59 created a real advantage for us, becoming the "authority" in the room. At times, DoD folks would ask for the impact of a particular concession, and I punched it in, printed the offer sheet, and handed it to them. When we finished negotiations, they accepted our final offer with one condition. They wanted us to provide them with two TI59s and printers. We laughed, agreed, and shook hands to conclude the negotiation.

A Hard Lesson in the Auto Industry

I had just taken over as general manager of Texas Instruments' Manufacturing Automation Services (MAS) business in the 1990s, when I performed a project review on a program with one of the big three auto companies. The program was to design and install a new automated engine assembly plant in Michigan. It was on schedule, and TI had spent several million dollars designing the factory, gaining engineering approval, and purchasing and installing more than $3 million of equipment. We'd received written authorization to proceed from a company officer, but we hadn't received a purchase order when I took over the business.

I scheduled a visit to the company's Purchasing V.P. to receive the purchase order and present invoices for our costs to date. When we ar-

> Don't assume your predecessor cleaned out poorly-performing projects and correctly stated the financial risks.

rived at Detroit headquarters, we were led to a conference room and waited an hour for the Purchasing V.P. to arrive. When he finally breezed in, without even sitting down, he rudely told us he knew why we were there, and we had wasted a trip. I provided him with a demand letter and the customer's authorization letter, neither of which he read. He said, "Do you have anything in writing from Purchasing?"

I said, "No, but we have a letter from your V.P. of Engineering, which is legally binding."

He replied, scorn dripping from his every word, "You're big boys; you know better than to start work without authorization from Purchasing. Get your equipment out of our facility within thirty days or we'll sell it for scrap." With that, and not even so much as a goodbye, he walked out of the conference room. His assistant took us to the lobby, and we flew home.

Later, we discovered that the company had cancelled plans for the automated engine plant, and we had intentionally not been informed. When I returned to TI, I recommended filing a lawsuit, and our Legal Department's opinion was that we would prevail. It was irrelevant, however, since TI sold millions of dollars of semiconductors to the company each year, and my claim could endanger TI's other business with the company. My little MAS business had to absorb the loss, wiping out the entire year's profit and putting MAS on the road to closure.

While this disaster wasn't on my watch, it reinforced an important guideline. Do not start work on a project without either a contract or a binding agreement to fully reimburse your company for any costs expended. Your customer contact might be an ethical person who intends to do what's right if the project is cancelled, but what happens if he/she is reassigned and you're forced to try to recover your costs from someone new?

Back to Texas

When I joined ADC Telecommunications in1998, the CEO agreed that once I had set up my organization and begun showing improvements, the company would pay to relocate Dottie and me back home to Dallas. I worked hard to meet the one-year goal, and in that time, I formed my new organization and aggressively at-

> Even when unpleasant, don't hesitate to ask people to honor their commitments to you. Be persistent.

tacked the challenges, demonstrating annual savings of more than $50 million. Although the CEO was not pleased when I raised the subject, he honored his commitment.

Dottie and I moved back to Texas in August 1999, and I moved into ADC's facility in Telecom Corridor in Richardson, a twenty minute drive from our new home in Allen. I hired an executive assistant, and we set up weekly long-distance staff meetings that proved to be a 1999-version of today's virtual officing. We used a portable videoconferencing system for meetings, and I stayed in touch with my staff while I was in Dallas. Even so, I traveled often to Minnesota for in-person staff and board meetings.

Effective Negotiations Training, Take Two

Toward the end of my time at Schneider Electric, I conducted a Lessons Learned conference focused on understanding and correcting the causes of a major project failure. We were discussing our relationships with the government customers, and I heard that our project team had been continually jerked around by customer demands for changes in designs, specifications, priorities, schedules, and personnel assignments. Our team members tried their best to accommodate the requests, despite the inefficiencies and confusion they caused.

I asked, "Why did you agree to change direction when you knew it would defocus the project team and cost time and money?"

The answer was, "Because they're the customer."

I asked, "Who is authorized to give program direction in the federal bureaucracy?" I was answered by a room full of blank stares.

I answered my own question: "The contracting officer is the only person authorized to give direction or make contract changes, and he or she jealously guards that authority. Why would you take direction from someone who has no authority, yet interferes with your project?" They began to understand the problem.

Next question: "How many of you have ever taken an effective negotiations training course?" Three hands went up in a room of forty senior people, including five V.P.s and many senior managers. In a company as large as SE, could it be possible that senior managers and executives had never been trained in the art and science of negotiations? Bingo, I had a target for improvement.

I asked my Purchasing Manager to investigate negotiation training courses, in particular the Chester Karrass "Effective Negotiations" course I'd taken almost forty years earlier at TI. She found that the Karrass course had been updated and was still offered routinely around the country. I asked her to attend a session and report back, which she did with glowing recommendations. We immediately planned a pilot course at our facility in Dallas, with thirty-nine participants, including executives, directors, and managers.

I sat in on the course, kicking it off and closing it with practical applications from my forty years of negotiating contracts in multiple businesses, industries, and cultures. I was pleased to find that the course was even better than my recollection of the class I took in 1977. Dealing with negotiation strategy and tactics, expectation management, and cultural negotiations, it had plenty of benefit for everyone in the room. Responses, even from the executives who attended, were overwhelmingly positive, and we made the decision to take the course to every customer-facing employee in SE's U. S. Buildings Business. Beginning in August 2012, we committed more than $100,000 for the training of more than 275 employees who touched customers. The results were excellent, with overall satisfaction scores of 9.2 out of 10 for "Quality of the Course," and 9.0 for "Value of the Course at This

> If you've never been formally trained in the art and science of negotiations, I recommend it.

Point in My Career." I kicked off and closed each class with practical applications and challenges to the participants.

Chapter Eight

Dancing With Your People

You gotta have fun in your work. The more you inspire your organization to work with joy, the better the results. Dealing with your folks on a human level is rewarding, as you inspire them to catch your vision and work with joy. But it's not always fun. Dancing can be painful!

The 100,000th Paveway

In 1980, Texas Instruments was approaching the delivery of the 100,000th Paveway Laser Guided Bomb, when we proposed holding a huge celebration. It was an easy sell to TI's executives, and we planned to commemorate the milestone with a party at our production facility in Sherman. We invited a large group of dignitaries, military executives, and TI executives. Paveway was the largest and most profitable program in the history of TI, and we really dressed up the facility. The 100,000th Paveway was identified, and on October 9, 1980 we had a great celebration. There were tours, dignitaries, good food, recognition of the entire Paveway team, and an open house for employees and their families.

Despite the cost and all the work involved, the event was great fun, giving tours and briefings, recognizing our Paveway team, and commemorating a hugely successful program that supported our troops for decades. A number of military dignitaries attended, including four-star Air Force General Alton Slay. TI's executive team was in attendance, including President J. Fred Bucy, and numerous V.P.s. A lot of "thank

yous" were given out, and we received great publicity. It was a
wonderful party and recognition
for the entire Paveway team. I'm

> Take time to celebrate your
> teams' successes.

proud to have invested almost ten years of my career in this outstanding
program.

Take time to celebrate your teams' successes, and say thank you to
them and their families for their sacrifices. Your folks are proud of their
work, and they want to share it with their families.

The Original Chicken Dance

In 1989, Bill Mitchell, then President of Texas Instruments Defense
Business, was on the Board of Directors of the Dallas County Community College District when a research center was built in south Dallas.
DCCCD was a large county college system with over 80,000 students.
The new facility was being named for Bill J. Priest, a popular, long-time
DCCCD manager, renowned for wearing a bow tie every day of his professional life. Bill Mitchell called me and explained that he wanted TI
to put on a show at the ribbon cutting ceremony, to be attended by local
dignitaries and media. He didn't know what he wanted, but he thought
it would be neat to include a robot somehow. The ceremony would be
outdoors under a huge tent, with a full complement of speeches and
congratulations. We had a number of robots in our Lewisville lab, so we
decided to do it up right.

We selected a large, six-axis, fully-articulated, single-arm robot for
the grand opening. With the arm extended vertically, the robot was elev-
en feet tall and weighed several thousand pounds. We painted it in TI
colors, added TI logos, a large bow tie, and huge scissors at the end of the
arm. It was programmed to move through a routine to demonstrate the
size, speed, flexibility, and agility of something that large. We developed
"The Chicken Dance," with fast-moving, sweeping, twisting, extending,
and collapsing motions, exercising five "joints" simultaneously. When it

> Employees love the opportunity to "strut their stuff," and their projects can be huge fun.

was cranked up, it looked like an insane chicken. Its last act was to cut the ribbon stretched across the stage, then take an elaborate bow. All this would be triggered by Bill Priest from the stage, where we put a switch box on the podium with a huge green button.

We pulled together DCCCD and construction personnel, shared our plan, and gave them our list of requirements. We moved the robot to the site in south Dallas, and poured a concrete slab for the robot's foundation. Since the location didn't have enough power to run the robot, we set up a long-distance feed from the main facility. We practiced and practiced, solving problems and refining the plan for two weeks. Our engineers had a ball; they had never done anything like this before (nor had I), and they really got into it. They put bells and whistles all over the robot, named it "Digger," and refined "The Chicken Dance."

The day of the grand opening was hot, and I was sweating bullets. I got to the site two hours early and met with the engineering team. They ran through the whole process, and it worked flawlessly. Everything was ready to go, right? Well, the best laid plans … the power supply blew up, and we had to scramble to get power re-established, then re-boot the robot.

We went into the ceremony very nervous, and when it came time for the ribbon cutting, Bill Priest pushed the button, and … everything went off like clockwork. It could have been a career-limiting moment, but it was so impressive that we got a huge ovation and great media coverage.

Anniversary Celebrations

For all the hard-work, Texas Instruments had a tradition of having fun when employees reached career milestones, and service recognition banquets were celebrated annually at all our sites. As the Lewisville, Texas Site Manager, I helped host the recognition events, including annual banquets for employees attaining milestone service anniversaries (twenty or more years). The banquets were attended by the executive team, which became the good humored target by the end

> Employees want to know you as more than a stiff-necked boss; making yourself human is a good thing.

of the evening. The banquets were eagerly anticipated, with an open bar, great food, and live entertainment that always included bringing executives on stage and making fun of them. I learned the benefits of "executive human-ness" early on, but as an introvert, it didn't come easily for me. By the late 1980s, I was responsible for more than 5,000 people on seven sites, and I did a lot of traveling to recognize employees and make myself more real than just a name. I had to learn to laugh at myself.

In addition to the annual events, the Lewisville management team enjoyed holding personal recognition events for senior managers, and I had planned and hosted a number of these events over the years. I enjoyed poking fun at others, especially executives.

In February 1988, my fifteen-year service anniversary, it was my turn. I knew something was being planned to get even with me for all the mischief I had sponsored over the years, but I had no idea what was to come. While the event was fun for the audience, it was pretty embarrassing for me, although I was grateful for the *400* friends who came out to help me "celebrate" my anniversary … and get even. The gifts were funny, including strange headgear, apparel, and communications devices, both real and contrived, and I had to wear them all day. Presenters took great joy in introducing each and every aspect of my new wardrobe, and dressing me in it. By the end, I was mostly-akin to a space alien, dressed to the hilt in crazy technology garb. My lovely wife and mother also participated by providing embarrassing photos of yours truly at various ages and in unglamorous settings and attire. While embarrassed, I was honored that so many friends and colleagues came all the way to Lewisville to recognize me.

Men in Black

In 2005, in preparation for a Schneider Electric Leadership Meeting in Dallas, our executive team put together a video for the conference. The day of the conference, the meeting room was packed with more than 100 senior managers. A screen came down, and our video started. The executive team was dressed in black suits, shirts, and ties, and dark sunglasses *a la* "Men in Black." The Black Eyed Peas song "I've Got a Feeling" was blaring while the video-execs in their offices lip-synched. Each got up and marched down the stairs to the front lobby. As the camera followed and the music blared, we got into cars, dancing and singing, and drove to the conference center. In the hallway the Men in Black executive team circled the camera with arms linked, the scene spinning. The circle opened, and the music volume dropped. I sauntered toward the camera, turned and looked critically at the execs in the circle. Following my disdainful survey of the executive team, I looked into the camera, and said, "You know the difference between all those knuckleheads and me? I make this look good." We turned and danced through the doors into the conference center.

> Humor is a powerful tool for setting the mood and encouraging participants to engage in, and enjoy, conferences.

At the point in the video when the doors opened, we entered the conference room in real life, dressed in our Men in Black outfits, and danced across the room. The video kicked off the highly-successful Leadership Conference on an upbeat, humorous note. Seeing the executive group in an informal skit was huge fun for our managers, and we had a productive strategy session. By the time the week was finished, everyone was on-board, and the video was so popular, we updated it a year later for a U.S.-wide technology conference.

Maddie Awards

At Schneider Electric, late in my career, I was successful building a team of talented people focused on improving business operations. Over six years, the group grew to more than thirty people, and as our credibility and success spread, the team was constantly in demand in the field to solve customer problems. Our team

> Recognizing your team and celebrating success is important. Even better, make it fun.

was comprised of experienced and energetic people who operated with customer focus, providing direct support to the business units and customers. While successful across the company, we also had a lot of fun and took advantage of the varied skills of our team in unique ways.

One of our most energetic members was Stephanie Kraemer, who was at the beginning of her very successful career. However, there was one concern. Stephanie was a bit shy, although she had all the skills to be successful. We needed to help Steph become more aggressive and outgoing, since leadership is not for introverts. One of my first actions, given Steph's quiet and unassuming demeanor, was to nickname her "Mad Dog." I don't think she liked it much at first, but as she began to experience success and gain confidence, her leadership really took off. She reminded me of a college graduate forty years earlier who made a conscious decision to change his personality to compete on the TI stage. We gave Steph the assignment of conducting a major negotiation with AT&T, and she delivered an excellent deal, saving the company a bucket of money. Mad Dog became a key part of our team, taking on the additional responsibilities for team recognition and communications.

In looking for a suitable way of recognizing Steph for her accomplishments, we developed an award, named in Stephanie's honor, that we gave to employees to recognize their work. Thus was born the Mad Dog Award, known as the "Maddie." It was presented using a Power Point file that began with a picture of the recipient which dissolved into a second picture, intended to represent the person's demeanor if pushed too far. These Mad Dog photos were often of enraged beasts or muscle-bound wrestlers, delivering on the Mad Dog challenge. Beneath the public demeanor of a Maddie is a backbone of iron and a personality intense enough to get the job done.

We had a lot of fun with Maddies at SE. At least, I had a lot of fun. Maybe some of our recipients didn't appreciate the whole depiction, but I can assure you the group got even with me when they found out I was retiring.

Chapter Nine

Building Something Intentional

O ver my career, I was directly or indirectly responsible for dozens of facilities projects, from simple office redesigns to huge greenfield real estate and construction projects. They totaled millions of square feet and more than $1 billion in construction costs. I've also been the "owner" of projects where I set the vision and design, support organizations executed the projects, and my organization occupied the finished facilities. The single largest construction project was ADC Telecommunications World Headquarters in Eden Prairie, Minnesota, a greenfield project with more than 500,000 square feet, costing just under $140 million. The art budget alone was more than $3 million. As TI Lewisville Site Manager, I was responsible for the 1.5 million square foot facility, and more than 5,000 employees, although many did not report to me directly.

Designing, building, and equipping facilities was a large part of my career, and I loved the challenge of creating a vision in response to a business opportunity, then putting together a team to fulfill that vision. This chapter is a short summary of lessons learned from the world of facility and factory design and construction ... and one tale of product design.

Paveway III Factory Planning

An industrial engineer by education and abilities, I loved the challenge of optimizing operations. As Texas Instrument's Paveway III

> Be willing to learn from anyone and everyone—competitors and allies alike. Different industries offer improvement ideas that you may have never dreamed of.

factory was being designed, we wanted to use the latest advances in automation and factory management, so six of our key managers made a weeklong trip to visit major production facilities around the country. Traveling on TI's company jet, we toured high-productivity factories in seven locations, all in a week. The private jet was a huge productivity boon versus commercial air travel, but it also had its drawbacks. It was a cigar with less than six feet of head room and seating for five. We squeezed in a sixth seat, rotating three travelers at a time through the back bench seat. Since several of us were large men, it was a pressed-ham experience on the back seat.

We learned a lot from the tour, especially our visits to Apple, Compaq, and Tandem Computer (Radio Shack's proprietary computer manufacturer, back in the day), where high-volume manufacturing techniques were used in the personal computer industry. Perhaps the greatest eye-opener was the state-of-the-art in warehousing and material handling, where automated warehouses, linked tightly to production planning systems, provided material to the shops without human intervention. The trip was quite an education in the late 1970s, and we used much of what we learned for our Paveway III factory.

If You Build it . . .
Maybe No One Will Come

In the mid-1980s, Texas Instrument's Defense business was growing rapidly with the Reagan Defense build-up and the monster successes of the HARM and Paveway programs. The 1.5 million square foot Lewisville site was bursting at the seams, and we'd already leased more than 100,000 square feet at another site. TI owned land up the road in Denton, Texas, a great community with two colleges and a well-educated populace. The site had been undeveloped for years, awaiting a suitable need for expansion to the site.

In late 1986, my team and I began designing an advanced engineering and manufacturing facility for the Denton site. It would be 380,000 square feet, in a modular design with pre-planned expansion capacity. The facility was designed with an advanced material han-

> Sometimes greatness dies due to no fault of its own.

dling system, employing below-ground tunnels linking the automated warehouse with every part of the site. Automated guided vehicles (AGVs) delivered materials all over the site, going up and down elevators automatically, and maintaining inventory control site-wide. It was a beautiful concept, and once again we received strong support from TI executives. Ground-breaking was in April 1987, and the site celebrated its grand opening in October 1988. A robot cut the ribbon to open the site, performed another chicken dance for the crowd, gyrating and swaggering in multiple directions at once, as only a robot can do.

In addition to the highly-advanced material handling systems, the site housed a number of unique facilities. Of particular interest was a large outdoor infrared-testing facility, allowing missile guidance systems to be tested on simulated targets. It's still there almost thirty years later.

The Denton site had a great run until the Berlin Wall fell in 1990, and the drumbeat to reduce defense spending began. It was only a matter of time before TI's Defense business was scaled back, and the Denton site was shuttered. It was open for five years, then remained empty for a number of years, eventually purchased by The University of North Texas for use as a research facility. I've driven by it dozens of times since, often wondering what happened to the material handling systems and all the bells and whistles we spent so much money on. Likely the people who work there now don't know the history, and I'm sure they puzzle over the amazing facilities.

Organizing a Strategic Operation

When I moved to Texas Instruments' Defense Suppression Division in 1983, I was challenged with designing and implementing a huge, classified manufacturing facility for high volume manufacturing of HARM missiles. It had to be strategic in vision, state-of-the-art in manufacturing, high-quality and -productivity, and successful for years in the future. The factory planning project involved hundreds of people across multiple sites. It was a complex task with a huge Gantt chart and a combined TI and DoD budget of almost $200 million. Our approach, beginning with a vision and cascading through all layers of planning and implementation, included multiple disciplines. For any major project, I recommend using the following planning process.

1. Organize the **Factory Design Team**, with clearly-defined scopes, responsibilities, and accountabilities.
2. Identify and empower a **Factory Team Leader**.
3. Implement an **Executive Steering Team** with overall integration responsibility.
4. Create a shared **Strategic Vision** with critical product and factory parameters.
5. Define the **three critical elements of any project: Scope of the project, Deliverables, and Acceptance Criteria.**
6. Plan for **Facility Constraints**, the high-cost/low-yield steps of the manufacturing processes.
7. Establish **Operational Guidelines**, including automation concepts.
8. Organize the entire **Investment Package** under a single capital investment umbrella.
9. **Design-in Flexibility** for continuous improvement.
10. Execute **Factory Implementation** with discipline and accountability.

11. Hold recurring **Design and Implementation Reviews** to ensure every organizations' buy-in and accountability.
12. Conduct a **Factory Test Run** under production conditions, collecting all data.
13. Formally **Approve the Facility,** validating it against the Scope, Deliverables, and Acceptance Criteria established in #5.
14. **Celebrate** the success.

For any large project, ensure you have executive support, adequate budget, strategic vision, a committed team, and an accountability process. Document the vision, design parameters, and team responsibilities and accountabilities. Brief your executives regularly to insure they provide needed resources. Ensure open communications by holding disciplined project reviews, with full documentation and communications up (and down) the management chain. Establish processes for decision-making, accountability, and reporting.

> Beware of the first rule of automation: "Never automate a bad process!" And its corollary, "Never automate production of a bad design!"

Turbochef

Not everything I did involved large-scale installations. Following my tenure in Texas Instruments' IT division, I was offered a General Manager position in the Custom Manufacturing Services (CMS) business. CMS performed contract manufacturing for companies that outsourced their manufacturing. After twenty years of service, I took over a start-up business opportunity with the objective of transitioning defense resources to the commercial marketplace. My new boss (George) was an old-school TI executive, hard-fisted and intolerant of anything that smelled the slightest bit like bad news. He was quick-tempered and used shouting and profanity as a leadership style. I actually liked him when he wasn't dealing with a problem, as he was quick-witted, knowledgeable, and friendly, but when he encountered a problem—especially a surprise—he went ballistic. The bearer of the bad news took a verbal beating, usually in public, until he was through reacting and ready to listen.

An entrepreneur I'll call Bill had come to TI looking for a partner to help bring his product to market. His company, Turbochef, produced a high-speed oven that used microwave cooking, high temperatures, and high-velocity air to cook food quickly in a fast-food restaurant environment. Bill brought his concept to the prototype stage using a local machine shop, but he needed help to qualify the design and take it into production. He had a meeting with George, and I was brought in to develop the program, qualify the design, and bring it into volume production.

Bill wanted TI to take an ownership interest in Turbochef, taking sweat equity as compensation—which my boss completely rejected. He gave me the job of proposing, negotiating, and executing a *profitable* Turbochef project, despite the uncertainty in the product design. Bill refused to pay what the engineering work was worth, but he finally agreed to a slimmed-down scope of work. He then did nothing but complain about cost and waffle on the design, putting me in a very uncomfortable position. I should have learned from my prior assignments, but I was following directions and trying to deliver a profitable business.

I brought a small number of Defense employees onto my Turbochef team, and when we signed the contract, I located the Turbochef business in the middle of a Defense facility. Redesigning the oven was tough, and it was required to undergo certification testing under UL, FDA, FCC, and other standards. The first customer was Pizza Hut, and the plan was to install two or three ovens in every Pizza Hut world-wide. This was the kind of production opportunity that was intriguing, if we could just get through the design and certification process.

Bill invited me to accompany him on a trip to Pizza Hut's headquarters in Wichita, Kansas, where I met the customer and learned about fast food restaurants. At the time, Pizza Hut was in a competitive fight with Little Caesar's Pizza, and they really took their competition seriously. As we drove to the front door of the Pizza Hut headquarters in Wichita, I saw a huge banner that hung from the top of the building all the way to the second floor, just above the front entry. The building was ten stories tall, and the lettering read, "We come to bury Caesar, not to praise him." How's that for an "in your face" strategy statement? I have used that example many times over the years when discussing strategy, competition, market focus, and employee motivation. It just doesn't get any more focused than that.

As we built the first ten Turbochef systems, we had to qualify the new design with real cooking. The oven cooked a perfect pizza *in less than a minute,* and a juicy chicken breast in less than two minutes, all automatically. When we were cooking, the wonderful pizza smell wafted over the entire defense facility, and at break times, people from all over the facility lined up to eat free pizza.

In early January 1993, I received a call from the senior business writer for *The Dallas Morning News*, who had gotten wind (or smell) of our Turbochef project. Following the fall of the Berlin Wall, he saw it as a positive story, transitioning defense resources to commercial businesses. TI was still an insular company, reluctant about engaging in PR work and distrustful of the media. I knew better than to just agree to the story, so I ran it up the chain to TI's PR department, hoping for a negative response. To my surprise, I got the OK to do the interview, which was really not what I was hoping for. I called Bill, and he was ecstatic about getting free publicity. He and I met with the writer and a photographer at our manufacturing shop, where he interviewed us for an hour and took pictures. We cooked pizzas and chicken breasts, and he went away excited about what he saw as a great story.

Over the next couple of days, we had several phone calls as he wrote the story and asked for elaborations. He sent me the article, and I found a number of errors. When I went through them with him, I only succeeded in making him mad. He said, "I don't need you to edit my writing." Now I was really concerned, because despite being the largest employer in the Dallas area and a great corporate citizen, there had been more than a few articles critical of TI. There was a distrust of the media at the highest levels of TI, just waiting to launch an "I told you so" if the story was negative.

Early the next morning, I was up and dressed before the newspaper arrived. When it hit the front sidewalk, I was on it like a duck on a June bug. I brought it inside and quickly pulled out the Business Section, which I went through twice without finding the article. I heaved a sigh of relief, thinking I had lived to fight another day, but when I dropped the paper on the kitchen table, the paper opened to the front page, and there, just below the fold was my smiling face. *Oh, no; not the front page!*

The article was actually quite good, and it got a good response within TI. I even received a phone call from a hard-nosed Executive V.P. He said, "Stewart, I'll be G** d*****. I work my *** off for thirty-five years, fighting for any kind of good press, and I open up the **** paper today and they're talking about a ******* pizza oven. I'm p*****." He hung up, and I took that for a compliment, coming from him. Maybe he was even trying to make a joke; I don't know, but I wasn't going to call him back for clarification.

This was before the Internet, but the story was picked up by AP, UPI, CNBC, CBS, *USA Today, New Edge News,* Reuters, and others, and it traveled around the globe in two days. Our PR department received calls from all over the world, and out of spite, they gave every one of the callers my phone number. I had to set up a database to track calls and follow-up actions. I had requests for interviews from newspapers, magazine editors, and radio stations, and although it was covered on local TV, I personally didn't make it on TV, thank goodness. We worked on stories with nine TV or radio stations, and dozens of newspapers world-wide, *in the first week,* and it went on from there. I had calls from Australia, wanting to know where to buy an oven, and another from Europe, wanting to buy stock in Turbochef. I had inquiries from entrepreneurs about building other products, and I became the target of prank calls, as well.

One of the local radio giants sent a reporter to interview me in our Defense plant, and this time it was fun, cooking pizza on the air and exchanging teasing comments about pizzas and bombs. The last part of the piece was the interviewer eating pizza and "OOHing and AAHing" over it. The interviewer's final question was how he could get one of those ovens. Sometimes, my big mouth exceeds the speed of my brain, and I have no idea where some of these things come from. My response was, "From what I can see, you don't need any more pizza." The station rolled in laughter for a while, and I thought the interviewer was going to choke to death before he could sign off. Why do I do things like that?

The oven certification process was difficult, meeting the standards of four different government and safety organizations, but we eventually passed and were ready to finish manufacturing and delivery of the first ten ovens. However, due to many mid-course, customer-requested design changes, design costs ran over budget. When I went to Bill with a request for him to cover the additional cost, he went ballistic and refused. I went back to George with the cost overrun, and he went ballistic. His instructions were to get the money back from Turbochef, with no alternative. I was stuck between a rock and a hard place, and I couldn't crowbar things back together.

My relationship with Bill became contentious when I continued to push to recover the design overruns. He went over my head with a demand that I be removed from the project. That was probably the best thing to do, since I wasn't getting any relief from either him or George. The decision was made to shut down the project after finishing the first ten ovens. We didn't leave Bill hanging, but we decided not to take the project into volume production. He found another manufacturer for the design that TI developed and certified, and the new manufacturer was able to reap the rewards of volume production.

Turbochef eventually went public, and Bill sold out and went on to other things. He benefitted hugely from our work on the design, certification, and pilot production, and he used us badly. Today, behind the counters of Pizza Hut and Subway restaurants nationwide, you'll see Turbochef ovens. I often pass their headquarters in Plano, and my thoughts are always the same, "I wonder what I could have done differently?"

The project was very challenging; bringing on employees on a short budget, and I wasn't able to promise them anything beyond a year of twelve- to fourteen-hour days. Turbochef became my final TI career assignment, and I found homes for all my people when the division was shut down. My last official act at Texas Instruments was to lay myself off after twenty-one years. I should have foreseen the risks of engineering overruns and protected the project with a cost-plus contract. Being between a hard-nosed boss and a cheap customer was impossible.

> Not everyone does business with the same degree of civility I was used to. I had to develop a thick skin and the ability to deal with harsh personalities and political posturing.

FSI Construction Projects

When I was V.P. of Operations for FSI International in the late 1990s, the company was expanding at a rapid rate, and the manufacturing facility was far too small and antiquated to handle the growth, cleanliness, and discipline expectations of our customers. The Board approved my plan to buy a piece of land in the area, and design and construct a high-tech, "clean" manufacturing facility. Using the same process I used in building the HARM manufacturing facility in the early 1980s, my team and I performed a "visioning" exercise to define long-term facility needs. We designed upgraded manufacturing facilities, added a Class 1 cleanroom lab, and included administrative and warehouse space.

Construction in Minnesota is difficult and restrictive, and environmental concerns trump all other factors. Our newly-acquired land was alongside a state highway, whose roadbed had been elevated a few years earlier. At the time, a culvert was installed under the highway at the south end of our property, allowing water runoff under the highway. Previously farm land, we intended to develop the entire site, but since the culvert installation, a small amount of water had drained onto our property and a wayward cattail seed drifted into the mud. On the overwhelming evidence of one solitary cattail, the area was proclaimed a "wetland," despite having been dry farmland a year earlier. We were required to completely redesign our site to provide permanent protection

> Construction projects can be high risk. Protect yourself and your projects with contingency plans.

for the "wetland." After months of redesign, we finally received approval to begin construction.

Our general contractor hired a "dirt contractor," but for some reason failed to require a performance bond. The dirt contractor wasn't in good financial condition, and when he didn't make payments to his truck drivers, they filed liens against our project. The dirt contractor skipped out, and we had to pay the subs and hire another dirt contractor. I was pretty upset, but somewhat mollified when, as part of the second "dirt deal," the new contractor let me spend an afternoon in the cab of an excavator, playing with big-boy toys, digging huge amounts of dirt and filling dump trucks. Now that's fun!

The completed facility fulfilled its vision beautifully: the Class 1 cleanroom laboratory functioned perfectly, the assembly and test facility was world-class, and the project finished on time and within budget, despite overruns on the dirt portion. The new facility helped elevate our corporate image, and it became an integral part of FSI's sales and marketing strategy. Once word of our new facilities got around, FSI was elevated to top-tier status in the tough semiconductor equipment market.

At the same time, we bought land and began construction of a new facility in Allen, Texas, for our Microlithography Division. It included an assembly shop, administrative space, and another Class 1 cleanroom laboratory. We located the project within the Allen Economic Development District, giving us special incentives to bring the facility to Allen. Once again, the project turned out well, and the 1997 grand opening was a special occasion.

ADC World Headquarters

ADC Telecommunication's World Headquarters planning was already underway when I joined the company as V.P. of Corporate Operatios in 1998. I took over responsibility for the multi-year project and moved quickly to identify a site and put together a capital package for the Board of Directors. The Board gave us the go-ahead, and we began the process of securing the site and putting detailed designs together. We bought land in Eden Prairie, next to a wetland, and negotiated financial incentives with the city and state for the development. The ADC world headquarters was a 500,000 square foot facility, budgeted to cost more than $140 million. We broke ground on the ninety-one acre site in early 1999, but the permitting process and dirt work took longer than planned, so we were stuck with very expensive winter construction. When I left ADC in 2001, the gorgeous facility was just coming on line, fulfilling its vision beautifully, but ADC's timing was terrible as the Telecom Industry was in the process of crashing.

We began work on another facility project in Allen, Texas in 2000, at the height of the telecom bubble. I got approval from the Board to build a greenfield facility to accommodate growth plans for the Broadband Systems Division. We found a nice piece of land on Highway 75 in Allen, a quarter of a mile south of the FSI International facility I built in 1997. We negotiated an incentive agreement with the City of Allen and began architectural and construction planning before the land purchase was complete. The site plan called for a 169,000 square foot campus capable of supporting long-term growth, and as we neared the closing date, I was at our broker's office on a conference call with the owner when I received a call from Bill Cadogan, ADC's CEO. I took it in the hallway, where Bill told me that recent forecasts were showing degradation in the telecom market, and he wanted me to pull the plug on the deal, even after receiving Board approval two months earlier.

We were already so far downstream, with so much time and money expended on the project, that I felt ethically obligated to finish the land purchase. He agreed, with the condition we cancel the project immediately following land acquisition. A few days after closing the land deal, I instructed our broker to begin the process of listing and selling the property. Announcing to the project team that we wouldn't be going forward with the project was a major disappointment and embarrassment. I personally met with the construction team to apologize and reassure them they

> Strategic relationships in the business world are based on mutual trust. If you're going to be a leader in the community, you must consistently demonstrate ethical behavior.

wouldn't be left holding an empty bag. They appreciated my honesty, and we negotiated termination agreements, although we probably could have terminated the relationships without having to pay the contractors. I remembered how I was treated by the Detroit auto company eight years earlier, and I determined I wouldn't behave that way. I felt an ethical obligation to compensate team members for the work they had performed.

The land eventually was sold back to the prior owner at a loss to ADC, and he went on to execute a grand vision for the property: a high-end shopping area, with boutique shops, classy restaurants, condominiums, and park areas.

At times it felt like whenever I undertook a major facility development project, there was an industry downturn that created affordability problems just as the multi-year projects were completing. I learned the value of maintaining strong executive support for my projects, and I stayed in touch with my CFOs to be sure there were no storm clouds gathering on the horizon.

When forced to cancel a project, it's important to do so transparently, and compensate your team members for their work. Maintaining good relationships with local businesses and governmental bodies is not only the ethical thing to do, it's mandatory if you want to do business in the community again.

Construction Management and Special Conditions

Within the construction process there are many unexpected issues that can arise and affect your projects. Several were unique to Minnesota and more stringent than we were used to in Texas. So, this is a short list of problems that impacted our projects ... probably not unique to cold-weather climes, but some were new to me.

Project approval processes are intricate and sometimes counter-logical. Watch out for regional planners who control development in the area. Their authority can cut across municipal boundaries, with the power to approve infrastructure expansion region-wide. Local zoning and state planning factors must be considered, so be sure to communicate closely with local governments to gain their support and prevent late surprises. Wetlands require special consideration, since obtaining development approvals in the vicinity of a wetland can be a major challenge. If you're perceived to have infringed on a wetland, you must be prepared to remediate the "damage." Also, water tables can sit at unpredictable levels, and a facility can affect the ground enough to change the surrounding water table.

> Facilities projects are exciting, but you must stay engaged and cautious to protect your interests. The construction industry is not universally ethical.

Cold weather construction is brutal. Wrapping a multi-story building in plastic, paying thousands of dollars per month to blast warm air throughout the building, and executing the project in winter conditions, all create a huge burden. In northern climes, road restrictions in the spring of each year, known as the "frost-out" dates, ban heavy trucks on roads for several weeks each spring. Until thawing completes and water drains away from the surface, trucks are banned from running on the roads, unpredictably impacting construction schedules. And don't forget about labor laws, as unions are always a factor. Restrictions and right-to-work rules can impact your project in unexpected ways. Develop plans to effectively manage organized labor concerns.

Execute facilities projects using the methodology I outlined in the first segment of the chapter, including a "dry run" of the facility before anyone moves in.

Chapter Ten

When Good Stuff Happens

There are times in everyone's life when good things happen. The unexpected times are the best. Whenever something rewarding happens that allows you to enjoy the successes of your life, you should take time to absorb and enjoy them. Don't feel you're unentitled, just enjoy them. And resolve that the special times in your life are instructive as you consider those who work with and for you. Positive recognition, especially unexpected recognition, is so rewarding. I commend it to you without reservation.

Wedding Party Guest

My fiancée, Dottie Coke, and I had set our wedding date for June 2, 1973, just over three months after I joined Texas Instruments. The lead-up to the wedding was a whirlwind, with non-stop preparations. And let's just say that you can get tired of parties, even when they honor you. Our pre-wedding parties were mostly at the houses of Coke family friends and business associates. We endured seventeen of them in two months, most of which are today a blur. However, one in particular holds a special memory for me. Late in the evening, I walked out to the backyard to enjoy a few minutes of quiet beside the pool, when an older gentleman walked up, introduced himself, and struck up a conversation. His name didn't register, but he knew who I was. He was one of the most interesting men I've ever talked to, and we spent quite a bit of time discussing a number of subjects. Unlike many successful people, this gentleman was genuinely interested in a twenty-two-year-old graduate and his opinions. What a neat gentleman. After more than fifteen minutes, we finished our conversation, shook hands, and returned to the house. I was sur-

> I wanted to be recognized as a stable and effective manager, known for relationship-building and providing support to others.

prised that in that entire time, no one had interrupted us.

My future brother-in-law, walked up and asked, "So, what did you and the mayor talk about?"

I said, "What do you mean?"

He responded, "That man you were talking to is the mayor of Dallas, Eric Jonsson."

I was floored for several reasons. First, he was the mayor, taking time to attend a party honoring us, not trying to impress anyone. Second, he took the time to really talk with (and listen to) a young person, genuinely interested in what I had to say. Third, he was humble. Fourth, he was Eric Jonsson, one of the founders of Texas Instruments, and though I hadn't been at TI long enough to know its history, it was terrific that someone with his credentials was so personable.

As my management style developed over the years, I often found myself thinking back to that evening and that gentle, humble man. I decided that was the type of leader I wanted to be. Beginning with the desire to be a good listener and humble learner, I wanted to be recognized as a stable and effective manager, known for relationship-building and providing support to others.

Executive Recognition

I had been managing Texas Instruments' Paveway programs in Sherman, Texas, for a year or so, and we were having phenomenal success, when I had the unexpected privilege of having the V.P. of our Defense Business come to *my* office to see me. Pat Weber was an outstanding

leader, but I'd never spent any time with him one-on-one. I was working in my office, when he came to my door and asked if he could come
in for a minute. He began, "Dr.
Stewart, how's it going here in
Paveway land?" I mumbled a response, totally surprised by his
unexpected visit. I'd had limited
interaction with him, but this
time he wanted to see me about
something important. He began
by explaining that TI's compensation system allowed for a few exceptional employees to be recognized for their (team's) performance. He
went on to say I was being given an incentive award, a stock option that
vested in three years, designed to provide incentive compensation. The
award was nice, but knowing that Pat had taken time from his busy
schedule to travel to Sherman and personally present me with the award
was the most important part of the recognition. I floated through the
rest of the day, unable to tell anyone at work, waiting impatiently to get
home so I could tell my wife, Dottie. I'm pretty sure I wasn't the only
person in Sherman receiving an award that day, and I learned later that
they were annually available at the executive's discretion to be distributed
as he/she saw fit. In fact, I remembered this occasion so clearly and positively that I made it a point to use exactly the same process when I was
presenting awards to my own exceptional performers a few years later.
What a boost for a new manager!

> Incentive compensation is
> a powerful form of recog-
> nition for your folks, but
> giving them your personal
> time and recognition is
> most important.

Halloween Celebration

By 1980, my leadership style had loosened a bit and become more
personable. I enjoyed the give and take that comes with an inclusive,
informal management style, but there's a potential downside that comes
when you open up the work environment. Giving your folks the authority to interact with you in an informal manner sometimes means having

to deal with teasing or difficult questioning. At times it can be downright embarrassing, but it's still the right way to go.

At Texas Instruments, the days before holidays and Halloween were relaxed, and work groups brought food to enjoy team meals. Despite losing productivity, those days were good for morale and teamwork, and we encouraged them. I enjoyed making the rounds on those days, sharing personal, spontaneous time with my folks.

One Halloween went over the top, and the joke was 100 percent on me. Some of our production folks enjoyed dressing up a bit on Halloween, and things could get amusing at times. At break time, I came out of a meeting on a short cycle to get to my next meeting. I needed to make a pit stop, after which I headed down the hall at a high rate of speed, head down and mind already on the next meeting. I rounded a corner next to the restroom and ... ran head-first into the waiting arms of a huge, hairy gorilla! It was at least seven feet tall! To this day, I have no idea who was in the suit. It encircled my head with huge, hairy arms, and began squeezing me in a giant gorilla hug. I was scared witless, and instantly reacted in a fight or flight reflex. By the time it turned me loose, the whole place was bedlam. The prank had been executed perfectly.

> It might be embarrassing, but when the joke's on you, grin and bear it. Everyone likes working for real people who value them and aren't afraid to laugh at themselves.

The production folks were on a break, so there were more than 200 witnesses, and the hootin' and hollerin' went on for some time. It took a while for my adrenaline levels to return to normal, and I had to put my hands on my knees and force myself to breathe normally. My head finally cleared, and when I looked up, the gorilla wanted another hug, this one a bit less gorilla-ish. The laughter rolled on, pictures were taken, and I never lived it down. For years, when I bumped into someone who had been there, I was reminded of the prank, and he/she enjoyed reliving the moment. All I could do was grin ruefully, and admit they got me good.

Dean Clubb

Dean Clubb was my boss during my time with Texas Instruments' HARM plant, and he was one of the finest communicators I've ever met. He could defuse a tense situation and keep even the worst disagreements from going critical. Dean had a library of colloquialisms, some of which provided comic relief. When someone took a stringent position, he would say, "You've got your chastity belt cinched up so tight you're likely to choke to death." Or when he needed to talk to someone, he'd say, "Shuffle cheeks on over here." If someone was unsuccessful in an assignment, he "took a pirouette on his pud." When it appeared Dean was on the wrong side of a dispute, he would disarm a tense situation by saying with a smile, "Boy, that took an ugly turn, didn't it?" I wish I'd had Dean's skills when dealing with some of the difficult people in my career.

> Candid conversation, mixed with humor, is an effective way to disarm a tense situation. If agreement isn't possible, at least part with a hand shake and an agreement to disagree.

Diplomacy is a skill that you need to learn at an early age. It took me far too long to learn it, and my hot-headedness got in the way at times. I eventually found that candid conversation, mixed with humor, was the most effective approach. If agreement wasn't possible, we'd at least part with a hand shake and an agreement to disagree. And if you have to go over someone's head, you need to tell him that's your next step, so he can't claim to have been blindsided. Know that you won't win every time, and be prepared to lose gracefully, living to fight another day.

Major Promotions

After my promotion to Operations Manager for the HARM program in 1983, and challenged with building and equipping my new organization for its coming enormous successes, I learned about executive compensation in a way I didn't expect. I reported to Bill Mitchell, S.V.P. of TI's Defense Suppression Division, but he was gone most of the time and I hadn't really gotten to know him well. He came in my office one day with a piece of paper, and proceeded to tell me I was being promoted two levels to recognize my new challenges. The job grade jumps came with a

> You never know when you might receive an un-expected promotion; just remember that others are always watching.

huge compensation increase, and I was surprised, since I thought I was already well compensated. I thanked him, and Bill went on his way.

Thirty minutes later, he came back and asked for the paper back. When I gave it to him, he hastily scribbled something else on the form … it was a promotion to Key Job status that hadn't been on the prior form. I found out later that TI's Executive Group was preparing for some huge executive changes, in which Bill would ascend to President of the Defense Business, and Dean Clubb would be promoted to Bill's prior position, S.V.P. of the Defense Suppression Division. When that happened, I got a new boss and was given an expanded role to Operations Manager of the entire Defense Suppression Division, which included multiple sites, and a number of "black world" classified projects that I didn't even know existed. All part of a major leadership realignment, and a great opportunity for me. It turned out to be a huge success path for my career, lasting almost ten years as the business grew enormously.

Upward Management Challenge

At the end of my time in Sherman, I ran Texas Instruments' Paveway Laser Guided Bomb operations with more than 400 employees. In a streamlining move, TI merged Air Traffic Control Radar (ATC) programs under me, including engineering and full P&L responsibility. Altogether, I managed $250 million of annual sales and more than 500 employees.

Bill Steele was manager of ATC programs, and he was twenty years my senior. He should have gotten the job—his job grade was two levels higher than mine. One of my first challenges was to tell Bill his job grade was being reduced. Bill was a first-class person in all regards, and he handled the situation professionally and unemotionally. If he resented me in my new role as his boss, he never let on, and we had a friendly and professional relationship, even to the point of sharing discussions of faith. I was uncomfortable, having a more senior manager reporting to me. I learned much from Bill, watching him work. I helped him when he asked for it, but otherwise left him alone to run his business. It was uncomfortable for me, but when I told Bill about it, he helped me with my awkwardness and taught me about "the high road." Thank you, Bill. I hope you are able to read this and hear my appreciation. What a great leader.

> **When faced with the challenge of taking over management of senior managers, be honest, direct, and supportive.**

FSI Supplier Conference

After leaving Texas Instruments in 1994, I went to FSI International, a semiconductor equipment company that was working hard to elevate its image and take on a first-tier role in the industry. With significant growth ahead of us, Tom Longmire, Director of Purchasing, proposed an FSI supplier conference to host key suppliers, share our growth plans, and develop strategic relationships that encouraged their investment in our business opportunities. I enthusiastically agreed, and Tom accepted the challenge and put together a fantastic initiative.

Our new Minnesota facility had been commissioned, and we held the conference there to show it off. It was a great day, strengthening supplier relationships and demonstrating our strategic value as their customer. I gave the keynote address, and it was a good speech, *until I got to the punch line*. It was a simple joke, about Texas Aggies flying an airplane, and the punch line was supposed to be, "Man, that is a really short run-way, but look how wide it is." I blew it, saying, "Man, that is really a wide runway, but look how long it is." The audience didn't respond the way I expected, and I immediately realized my error, dropped my head, then tried to recover.

Attempted recovery, "You know, the last thing my wife said this morning was, 'Whatever you do, don't screw up the joke.' I blew it. So, let me try again. Man, that was a really short runway, but look how wide it is." The audience laughed, but I lost momentum. Later in the agenda, when I came back on stage to make an introduction, I opened with, "But look how wide it is." The audience laughed for quite a while after that one, reacting to an Executive V.P. admitting an error and making fun of himself. My "humanness" earned me some points with the audience, and a number of folks came to me at a break with good humored jabs. The conference was a huge success, helping establish FSI as a major player in the tough semi-conductor equipment industry, and I earned a number of good friends as a result.

> Even in the most formal settings, showing an informal, humorous, and human personality is an engaging trait.

Involving your key stakeholders (suppliers, customers, employees, and executives) in a strategic planning conference is an initiative that can pay huge dividends. Well done, all attendees will leave the conference with a strengthened commitment to your vision.

The Ultimate Compliment

I recently had lunch with a long-time friend from my days at Texas Instruments, as well as later at FSI International. I don't want to embarrass him so I won't use his name, but he gave me the greatest compliment of my career. I value what he said above recognition I've received anywhere else. He had become extremely successful, rising to an execu-

> The most fulfilling feedback you will ever receive is from those people you've helped.

tive position with a global energy company, and I felt so good that I had known him "way back when." At lunch that day, we were reminiscing about the old days, and our times working together, and he said, "I owe everything I've achieved in my career to you." He became emotional, and said, "Thank you."

I wasn't anything more than a co-worker. He was one of those folks you knew would be successful. He'd gone far behind anything I could have taught him, and he is truly a world-class executive. That day, what he said to me, was emotional for me, too, and helped me feel as if I had fulfilled something special in my career. I truly appreciate his wonderful compliment, and I will cherish it forever.

Chapter Eleven

Leveling Up

Moving up in the corporate world is a function of hard work, acquired skills, demonstrated performance, and opportunity. I was never able to point at any one factor as the reason I received a promotion, but a combination of factors usually gained the outcome. Three of the four factors are self-evident, but opportunity is a function of timing and outside factors. Whatever the cause of the "right place, right time" event, you must be ready. That's not to say you'll always *feel* ready for the promotion, but what your bosses saw in you convinced them that you were, and it's your job to deliver on their expectations.

I've been asked how I progressed so quickly, moving through seven job grade levels and achieving "Key Person" status at TI in less than ten years. As I think back on those years, I'd have to say the key elements of my rapid career growth included intentional learning and change, the intentional excellence of constant innovation and improvement, integrity, determination and hard work, and recruiting and leading high-performance teams. I always enjoyed taking on new challenges, and I never said "no," a trait that would later get me in trouble.

My First Promotions

In 1973, after six months at Texas Instruments, I received my first performance review and got an unheard-of twelve percent salary increase. At the same time, in addition to my Paveway responsibilities, I assumed Production Control responsibilities for another product line, the Shrike missile. It was a classified program, behind locked doors, with a controlled work environment and stringent manufacturing standards. There were more than 100 assemblers on two shifts, ten dispatchers, and a large material kitting function. I managed both Paveway and Shrike operations for a year before adding a third manufacturing area to my responsibilities.

> It's always better to lead than follow. You'll have the initiative, and everyone else will be reacting to your leadership.

The Harpoon missile system, with more than 100 assemblers and twelve dispatchers on three shifts, was located in a different building. A few months after that, I added the Special Weapons manufacturing facility to my organization. Looking back, I realize I was quickly gaining experience and a strong reputation, and things were going very well. Leadership was becoming easier for me, I was young and had lots of energy, and I was willing to work hard to invest in my career.

With few exceptions, it's always better to lead than to follow. Career progress can come quickly when you put your head down and push forward aggressively. I didn't ask for these promotions or additional responsibilities, but I viewed them as opportunities and was ready when they occurred.

Stepping Up To Management Level

I was recognized for my work quickly, and three years later, I was offered a promotion and relocation to Texas Instruments' plant in Sherman, Texas, fifty miles north of Dallas. The entire Paveway Program was moving to Sherman where a major factory build-up was underway to start production of the second generation of LGBs (cleverly named Paveway II). Since the second generation system was going into production for U.S. forces, the prior version, Paveway I, had been authorized for sale to foreign allies through DoD's Foreign Military Sales (FMS) office. It was my first management position, and I would be the Paveway

I Manufacturing Engineering Manager, a combination of Project Management, Manufacturing Planning and Support, and Materials Management.

After a pizza dinner, my wife Dottie and I decided to accept the promotion, sell our house,

> Consider the impact on your family when offered a promotion. Moving, selling your house, changing schools, and a million details are stressful.

and move the family to Sherman. Dottie says I always delivered relocation decisions over a pizza dinner; this was the first.

Wearing Many Hats

My new assignment at Texas Instruments required me to wear three hats. The first was managing the Paveway II Tooling and Test Equipment project, a $30 million program which equipped TI's facilities with production tooling and test equipment. The second was the Paveway I FMS project, a $38 million production contract that ran for three years. The third was Paveway's Logistics Programs, a $20 million annual line of business that represented my first job as a P&L manager. For all three programs, I had great bosses who gave me incredible autonomy to develop innovative manufacturing technologies, lead high-performance teams, and execute production contracts.

Starting the new organization from scratch in a new city, we began building a team that could spread itself across the broad demands of our multiple assignments. It was at this time that I made the single best hire of my career. OK, so I didn't actually *personally* hire Tom Longmire, but he had applied for a job at TI, and he came to me when he reported to work. Little did I realize that working with Tom would be a great investment in *my* future. Tom had recently left the Army, and he hit the ground running. He was such a proactive, bright, and hard-working person, always able to anticipate issues and resolve them before they became crises. He's the finest negotiator I've ever known, and he was a major part of the huge successes Paveway enjoyed over the next decade.

The Paveway I and II projects required separate administration, since they were for different customers. The DoD's FMS Office had accumulated the Paveway I order for almost 5,000 systems, plus numerous types of test equipment, spare assemblies and parts. Logistically, it was a nightmare due to the eight countries involved. Deadly enemies were being armed with the same advanced weapons, under the same contract. We had to ensure there were no international problems during production and delivery, and I hate to think what might have happened if Iraq, Iran, and Israel discovered we were providing advanced technology weapons to their enemies.

> There's nothing better than leading a high-performance team, focused on shared objectives, stretching beyond your comfort zone, and enjoying success.

Middle Management, Here I Come!

After working six years in Texas Instruments' Sherman plant, taking on more responsibility and enjoying multiple promotions, in mid-1983 I received a call from Phil Gray, V.P. of Defense Manufacturing. Phil was the manufacturing executive and godfather of all Operations personnel within TI's Defense business, so he had a say in who got promotions and new assignments. Phil was a gruff bear of a man who took no guff from anyone. When he called, it was unexpected. He said, "Stewart, this is Gray. Your next job is in Lewisville. Call Bill Mitchell to find out what the job is." I tried to ask some questions, but he wasn't forthcoming, and that was it.

By 1983, I was leading all Paveway Operations and ATC Radar programs. Our team had designed and built the production facility for the next generation LGB (Paveway III, official name Low Level Laser Guided Bomb). While still producing Paveway I and II systems for delivery to U. S. and international countries, we implemented a new $100 million facility, including major factory automation and high-productivity processes. Production started up on time and budget, and the greenfield design and implementation project was a huge success.

With those successes behind me, at thirty-three I was transferred to the Dallas area to take over the role of Manufacturing Manager for the HARM (High Speed Anti-Radar Missile) Program. Once again there was a huge factory to be designed for a new weapon system, and I was tapped to lead the program. This one was tougher—a far more complex and expensive system with advanced technologies. Three experienced manufacturing managers in the division had worked on the HARM program for years, each of whom expected to get the job. Although I was an outsider, I was promoted over them. I knew little of the HARM system, but I was getting the job they thought they deserved.

Following meetings with Bill Mitchell, S.V.P. of TI's Defense Suppression Division, and my mentor, Jim Houlditch, S.V.P. of Defense Operations, Dottie and I had our pizza dinner, and I accepted the position. I began commuting to Lewisville immediately, a daily drive of more than 100 miles. Sherman had been a great place to live, and my career had really blossomed due to Paveway's "home run." Our kids were in elementary school, and though they were sad to leave their friends behind, moving to Plano would become a very good decision for our family.

Designing, building, equipping, and staffing the HARM Manufacturing Facility was the largest challenge I'd ever taken on. While the staff I inherited was a capable group of senior managers, they had no experience with volume production of complex systems. I was resented initially, because the three incumbents were all more senior, but what they didn't have was experience in factory planning, automation design, high-volume manufacturing, and strategic manufacturing.

The factory delivered on its challenge, starting up in an orderly fashion, and producing high-quality and –volume missiles on budget and on schedule. Within two years, I had picked up the additional roles of Defense Suppression Division Operations Manager and Lewisville Site

Manager, with 1.5 million square feet of facilities and more than 5,000 employees. At its peak, my Operations organization spanned six sites,

> Recruiting and leading high performance teams against major challenges provides career fulfillment like none other.

included more than 5,000 employees, and supported annual revenues of almost $1 billion. Job grade promotions and financial rewards came quickly, and I'm thankful for the outstanding teams I led. Their acceptance of my leadership and our shared vision provided a challenging, rewarding, and fulfilling assignment. Those years working on HARM were the pinnacle of my TI career.

Motorola Beckons

In 1988, I was contacted by an executive recruiter for a job opportunity with Motorola in Scottsdale, Arizona, as V.P. of Operations for a Defense Division. Initially, I wasn't interested since I had a great job at Texas Instruments and we were well-settled in our community. But as the recruiter talked about the opportunity, it sounded interesting. The phone interview with Motorola's VP of HR went well, and I was invited to Scottsdale for a round of interviews with the executive team. When I discussed the opportunity with my wife, Dottie, she was pretty closed to the idea, but we agreed it couldn't hurt to explore the waters a bit.

The trip went well, and when I met with the S.V.P. we hit it off. On the spot, he invited Dottie and me for an extended visit. I was convinced there was no way Dottie would consider a move to Arizona, but the opportunity for an expense-paid trip to Scottsdale was inviting, and she agreed to go.

It was a marvelous trip; I had a great visit at the plant, while Dottie went out with the S.V.P.'s wife to see the area. On Saturday, our tour of the area was beautiful, and we saw some wonderful neighborhoods. The S.V.P.'s house was in the low mountains outside Phoenix, an arid and beautiful area overlooking the desert. His backyard included mature citrus trees, all bearing fruit at that time of year. Our dinner was outstanding, with great company and a really nice bottle of wine. At the end of the evening, the S.V.P. told me he wanted me to come to Motorola, and he would be putting an offer together early the next week. We finished the weekend and came home, carrying backyard fruit home with us.

I was sold when we left Arizona, but there was no way I was telling Dottie that. I knew she wouldn't leave family, friends, and church, and I wasn't about to force a change like that. I didn't even get the chance to open the discussion. As we flew home, she said something like, "I could really enjoy living in Scottsdale. Do you think they'll make a good offer?"

It was, in fact, a great offer, including a substantial pay increase and an executive position, with significant growth potential over a short time. Dottie and I decided to talk to the kids, convinced there was no way they would be interested in moving to Arizona. We wouldn't force the issue with our kids, thirteen and eleven at the time, so it was likely a moot point. Wrong again. We sat down with the kids, showed them pictures of Arizona, ate the fruit we brought back, and then casually asked how they might feel about moving to Arizona. I almost fell out of my chair when they both said, "Wow, that looks really cool. When can we go?" Uh oh!

That was Friday, and I owed an answer to Motorola on Monday, so the weekend was nerve-wracking, considering a change after working only one place in my fifteen-year career. The family was firmly behind me in the decision to move. I told them we'd make a final decision Sunday over lunch after church.

I thought it was a done deal, but God had other plans. I don't remember the subject of the sermon that Sunday, but I'm convinced He spoke directly to me through it. He used that Sunday morning to impress me with the role He had for us in Texas. So at lunch I told the family I felt God wanted us to stay where we were, and that He had plans for us in Plano. They accepted the decision, saying they were happy to stay where God wanted us. I can't explain how I'm sure the message was so crystal clear, but I'm convinced it was the right decision. That was that, until I finally exited TI in 1994.

The Lord has a plan for your life, and listening to His direction will give you assurance of the purpose for your life. You'll become a better manager when you have confidence in your future. If there's a God-sized hole in your life, with confused priorities and direction,

> Always leave room for the Lord to act.

and a feeling of being lost, I encourage you to find a place to connect with your Creator. Don't look back; it will change your life ... personally, professionally, and spiritually.

Promotions

As you ascend the ladder, some opportunities can come with warts. You'll want to be discerning of the situation you'll be moving into, as well as an understanding of how long you'll have to deliver expected results. I received promotions twice where my "good soldier" mentality drove me to accept a position that was a bad idea in the end. I can directly trace my most painful career experience to a job I shouldn't have accepted, but that's hindsight.

Thinking back on the corporate ladders I traversed in my career, those in the first fifteen years came very quickly and with great rewards, both financial and job satisfaction. They fall under the category of organizational promotions, meaning the company promoted me continually to take on more responsibility and challenges. It was a great time for me and my career. The next fifteen years brought a series of senior management opportunities and executive and entrepreneurial moves that stretched me into new and educational roles. The endings were sometimes not of my choosing, but each one helped me grow in leadership skills and personal integrity. The last years of my career were intentional and fulfilling, pursuing excellence and reflecting my desire to make a difference in other people's lives. This was no longer a time of "climbing;" rather, it was a time of enjoyment of my career. Taking some corporate bows, doing things I enjoyed, and exiting intentionally, gracefully, and on my terms.

Over my career, many of the promotions and rewards I received were unexpected. The best ones were the surprises, whether a promotion delivered by the boss, an incentive award delivered by a S.V.P., or a change in career direction. Even when you think you're being taken for granted, people are always watching. I've been humbled a number of times over the years by running into people who remember me from earlier times. I may not have recognized them, but they remembered me, having a story or observation of something I did or said, and I'm grateful I hadn't behaved badly. Even when discouraged about your career, keep your head down and bust your butt. People are watching to see how you handle adversity as well as success, and everyone has failures at times in their lives.

Leaving the Defense Business

In early 1990, I once again received a completely unexpected call, this time from Texas Instruments' E.V.P. Bill Mitchell, to come see him about a new job. TI's Defense Business was down-sizing, and Bill and TI's Executive Committee wanted someone with Operations experience to lead the company's global manufacturing IT systems. At the same time, there was a desire to open a new line of business around TI's factory automation expertise. I got the call because of my experience designing, installing, and operating advanced factories. It was flattering to be selected for the position, but it turned out to be harder than I ever imagined.

TI had a fledgling $50 million Manufacturing Automation Systems (MAS) business, which implemented automated factory operations for large, high profile customers. In addition, several Information Technology organizations were brought together to form TI's Enterprise Systems Division. I was given responsibility for the new organization, reporting to TI's CIO, and I moved my office to TI's Plano facility.

As flattering as a promotion being offered by an executive vice president may be, never take for granted that what's being suggested is the best for you. Make sure your BS detector is working as the opportunity is being presented, although it can be a delicate decision to say, "No."

> New opportunities can come out of the blue, but some can carry high risk.

Enterprise Systems Business

Texas Instruments' computer systems were world-class, with global capabilities and talented people making the whole thing run efficiently. TI's IT excellence was exemplified by the company's self-designed global email capability in the early 1970s, far earlier than the Internet, and its home-written Material Requirements Planning (MRP) system. TI's global IT systems had been built from more than 100 million lines of hand-written COBOL code, giving the company a suite of systems that managed its global businesses, across dozens of countries. Amazing, but also far too expensive.

My new job was to pull together and manage several diverse organizations with multiple objectives. First was a global organization of 500 IT professionals providing manufacturing, materials, and support systems to the businesses of TI. There was also a fledgling $50 million external business, Manufacturing Automation Systems (MAS), whose charter was to sell factory automation solutions to large corporations. Although I don't know why, I also inherited a portion of TI's Central Research Laboratory, and I was further challenged to grow a second external business delivering TI's enterprise systems to large companies.

I was tasked to streamline the internal support organizations and introduce a culture of customer satisfaction, turn the external businesses profitable and grow them without investment, convert TI's IT systems into commercial products and begin selling them externally, and manage R&D activities focused on developing next-generation IT systems.

Chosen for this challenge because of my success with advanced manufacturing technologies, the executive group wanted to improve the return on TI's investments, improve customer service, and reduce the cost of the IT infra- structure. My first month was spent learning the business and building a vision for the new or- ganization. If I had it to do over again, I certainly would have been more pragmatic about the probability for success. I should

> When taking responsibility for a new organization, be brutally honest, and don't become enamored with an opportunity until you're confident your plan is vi- able and you have support up the chain.

have undertaken an immediate critical review of each organization, since there were major problems to be dealt with, some of which were hidden.

When taking responsibility for a new organization, you should al- ways perform a critical assessment of the viability of the organization. Identify hidden problems and bring them into the light of day, even to the extent of politely pointing the finger at your predecessors. Talk to leaders, key personnel, and customers, and perform financial reviews to gain a realistic view of the organization and your prospects for success. Be brutally honest, and don't become enamored with an opportunity until you're convinced it can be successful. Push your new boss to ac- knowledge your critical evaluation and give you a realistic opportunity for success, normally at least a six-month period to clean up any messes and begin delivering improvements. Be sure your boss will support you if you have to take aggressive action, and prepare a sixty day "Findings" report documenting the issues you uncover and your plan to resolve them.

Chapter Twelve

Battling the Octopus

Sometimes a bad idea takes on a life of its own, virtually impossible to kill. As you've no doubt detected by now, I'm not a fan of bureaucracies. Many of the events in this chapter were the direct result of giving too much authority to support groups, and losing focus on what's really important ... the customer.

Short-Sighted Management

On a trip to Houston in 1979, I visited Compaq Computer, a leader in the computer industry that was founded by a group of ex-Texas Instruments employees. They were very direct as they told the story of the founding of their company.

In the late 1970s, TI's Computer Division developed the TI Professional Computer (TIPC), an advanced machine that was the technological rival of any on the market. The design had been completed and validated, and leadership of the Computer Division met with TI's Executive Team for authorization to move into production. A critical decision was whether to use a "proprietary" operating system, or adopt the IBM operating system to deliver an "open" PC to the marketplace. If open, the TIPC could run any company's software, and TI software would directly compete with other software companies. A proprietary system allowed for more profitable software pricing, since it would be more difficult for others to write competing software for the TIPC.

TI executives were asked for the production go-ahead, and the development team recommended the open operating system (IBM Compatible). They received approval, but were told to go with the proprietary operating system. The development team leaders recognized the problem with that decision, and over the next

> Don't try to be everything to everybody. Focus on being the best: the concept of core-competency.

few months, most of the team resigned from TI and went on to open their own computer company. They used much of the TIPC design, but with an open (IBM-compatible) operating system. That new computer company was based in Houston and was named Compaq. Eventually, Compaq was sold to Hewlett Packard, and the founders became multi-millionaires, benefitting from a business that should have been TI's. Using the proprietary operating system, TI's PC business suffered poor acceptance and was shut down after a few unprofitable years.

TI's decision included an element of technical arrogance, focusing on technology as the objective and losing sight of customers' priorities. TI's primary strength was always technical innovation, but in my view, it lacked strong "productization" and marketing. I'm sure I'll get an argument from others who knew TI back then, but I watched the interaction with customers on too many occasions, trying to sell technology rather than solutions. TI had been consistently profitable and cutting-edge for decades, but it hadn't risen to the top echelon where a company with so much capability should be.

For years, TI's ambition was to be the largest semiconductor company in the world. The company was vertically integrated in order to control all aspects of its products. This meant investing billions of dollars in foundries and assembly and test facilities all over the world. When memory chips became commodities, the market required TI to operate on razor-thin margins. It was only after years of painful underperformance that TI decided it no longer wanted to be the world's biggest semiconductor company, but rather the most profitable. Under new executive leadership, the desire for vertical integration, requiring massive investments in operations that were not TI core competencies, came under intense scrutiny, and TI began divesting operations that were either unprofitable or non-core competencies. Today, TI is a more profitable and effective company, learning the lesson of focus. Don't try to be the expert at everything; you'll be spread too thin in capital, resources, and focus, and you run the risk of losing the ability to be best at anything.

Lubbock, Here We Almost Come

J. Fred Bucy was Texas Instruments' President, CEO, and Chairman in the mid-1980s, during the HARM missile production build-up. He was also on the Texas Tech University Board of Regents. At a regents meeting, the economy of the Lubbock area was discussed, and although TI already had a plant there producing semiconductors, computers, and calculators, Bucy decided it would be a good idea to move more operations to Lubbock. The HARM program seemed a likely candidate, with several thousand high-paying jobs, so he directed the S.V.P. of Facilities to investigate moving HARM to Lubbock.

The S.V.P. directed his team of managers to make it happen. I got a call from his V.P. of Facilities who opened the call with, "Stewart, we're moving HARM to Lubbock, and I need you to put together a transition plan." At first I was incredulous, thinking this had to be a joke. There were several thousand highly trained and experienced people in Lewisville who were fighting every day of their professional lives to execute the HARM program flawlessly, and it made zero sense to disrupt what we'd spent years building. Bucy, who was from Lubbock, felt it was a wonderful place to live, but Dallas-area employees who worked on HARM likely wouldn't share his enthusiasm.

The V.P. became irate when he detected I wasn't treating the issue seriously, and I finally figured out he wasn't joking at all. After the call ended, I called two levels up my chain of command, to Bill Mitchell, President of TI's Defense Business, who said, "No way. Just put together

a few slides that demonstrate how stupid the idea is, and we'll kill it."
One of my managers and I spent a couple of weeks working through the
financial, capital, program, and human impacts, and put it into a secret
package of ten slides.

I went to visit the S.V.P. of Facilities and his staff feeling I had an
ironclad case to kill the bad idea. He sat at the head of the table, and
when I started my briefing, he went to sleep. No kidding. I stopped, but
there were six other people in the room, including V.P.s, and one gave
me the "keep going" sign. For the next half hour, I briefed the room.
The S.V.P. woke up every so often, acted like he had heard everything,
listened for a few minutes, and dozed off again. I felt good that I had a
slam-dunk-winning argument, showing how the move would be a disaster. At the end of the briefing, I concluded with, "This is not a good
idea, putting the biggest program in TI's history at risk," I asked if there
were any questions.

The S.V.P. woke up, and thanked me for the briefing. No one else
in the room said a word the whole meeting. The S.V.P. said we'd begin
planning the move immediately. It was like he hadn't heard a word I said
(probably true since he was asleep most of the time), but more likely he
sat through my briefing already knowing the answer. He demanded a list
of requirements, then got up and left the room.

When I reported the outcome of the meeting to my bosses, Dean
Clubb and Bill Mitchell, they were livid. It was as though I had failed my
mission. They gave me the assignment to put together a full assessment,
then brief them and prepare for battle. We spent another two weeks
developing analysis after analysis until we were worn out. The Facilities
S.V.P. knew nothing about the HARM program and wasn't interested
in learning. His group fabricated data, absolutely certain they were on
the winning side. Their demands for a transition plan escalated, and I
got so frustrated I finally told Bill, "I can't win. I'm between you and the
S.V.P., and he feels he has a mandate from God to make this move happen." With that, Bill stormed out and demanded a meeting with Bucy,
where he told him the move would be over his dead body. Bucy, whether

> Strive to be known as a snake killer; someone who feels empowered to kill bad ideas and support customers.

truthful or not, retreated and said he was just asking the question, and had no intention of doing anything that might damage the HARM business. I have no idea how many hours of key people's time were wasted on this exercise, not to mention the stress. I was happy it was over, but it was just so senseless and wasteful.

I once read that Ross Perot, after joining the Board of General Motors, said something along the lines of, "At EDS, when we spotted a snake, whoever was closest killed the snake, and we moved on. At GM, when a snake is spotted, a committee is organized to study the snake, then it makes a recommendation up the chain on how best to deal with the snake. Months later, the snake is much larger and consuming large amounts of useful corporate resources and assets, and it's still not dealt with."

Sometimes a bad idea takes on a life of its own, virtually impossible to kill. Support groups that feel mandated and empowered can jeopardize a business in a heartbeat. Make sure you have an open communications channel far up the chain of command, to someone who can recognize a dangerous situation and kill it off, not to mention covering your back.

Insidious Culture

There are detrimental elements of our culture that insidiously intrude in your business, and you cannot turn a blind eye toward them. Like the gambling story from early in my career, drug abuse is a dark part of our society that ruins lives and can poison your operations. You must define your expectations and consistently enforce the provisions of your policies. This particular octopus is deadly.

Texas Instruments' Lewisville, Texas site housed more than 5,000 employees, and regardless of the level of security, the site had some of the same problems as the general population. In the late 1980s, we received a call from Lewisville police that they had information that drug trafficking was taking place on our site. I met with the chief, and we agreed to bring in an undercover officer to investigate. Over the course of a few months, he was able to establish contact with a

> Formal policies must be clear and unequivocal, and you cannot play favorites when there are violations.

drug ring operating on the TI site. He attended parties, observed drug usage, and bought drugs both on- and off-site. He gathered information on almost twenty TI employees, and arrested more than a dozen. If the cop personally witnessed a transaction or other crime, he arrested the person. Per TI's policy, the employee was suspended without pay, and if convicted his/her employment would be terminated. If the cop had only hearsay evidence, he didn't take direct action, but we called those employees in for drug tests. Some left the company, knowing they would fail the test, and others requested drug rehabilitation under the terms of our drug policy. We handled all the situations strictly in accordance with TI's drug policy, and in the end we lost thirteen employees.

Drug abuse is an insidious problem, and without swift, even-handed action, it will be a cancer on your organization. Your company must have a drug policy including provisions for rehabilitation support, disciplinary action, and termination. You cannot tolerate illegal activity in your operations, so make sure your investigations and decisions are thoroughly documented and corroborated by your HR and Legal Departments.

Squirrel Power

The 1.5 million square foot Texas Instruments Lewisville facility was designed with redundant power sources due to the need for 100 percent up-time for operations at the site. TI made a large investment in fully redundant power sources, and installed huge tanks on-site for emergency water and diesel fuel for electric generators. The redundant power inputs

> There are times when it's hard to fly like an eagle when you're surrounded by turkeys.

to the site were each capable of supplying emergency power in the event of a failure. So it was a huge surprise one day at 10:00 a.m. when the entire site went dark. Emergency lights came on, but normal operations, including air conditioning, shut down.

I was responsible for 5,000 employees, and it was my job to figure out what to do. The electric company didn't know what the problem was. They tried multiple re-sets with no success. After an hour, with 5,000 people away from their desks and milling around the windows, I made the decision to release everyone except the Facilities crew. Power didn't come back until late that night, so the decision to send everyone home turned out to be a good one.

The problem was traced to a power substation, where a squirrel had fallen into a transformer and shorted out the entire substation. In addition to turning himself into a crispy critter, he brought down a large portion of the City of Lewisville, including our site.

What about the dual power feeds, you ask? Shouldn't that have maintained power to the site even when one of the feeds went down? Good question, one I asked the electric company executives when we had a "come to Jesus" meeting.

Electric Company: "Yes, you have dual feeds coming into the site from different directions, but they both come from the same substation."

Me: "Huh, you mean we paid all that money for redundant power feeds, yet you tied them both back to the same substation? Where's our redundancy?"

Electric Company: "You have the two feeds you wanted."

Me: "What part of the word redundancy do you not understand?"

OK, I wasn't that sarcastic, but I was incredulous. Actions were undertaken immediately to bring a second feed to the site from a different sub-station. I don't think the electric company ever really got the point.

The Culture Wars

Two parallel organizations at Schneider Electric had longstanding differences, and it was a mutual problem. The Energy Solutions (ES) business was an organizational silo that evolved insularly over ten years under the leadership of its founder. The business had been successful, growing to more than $125 million of sales, but with a "stiff-arm" mentality that drove everyone else away. When I came on the scene in 2007, I was told by the ES executive to focus on other businesses, since his was performing so well. That lasted two years until ES came under financial stress. The V.P. refused to change and pointed fingers at everyone else until layoffs became necessary for the first time in history. The V.P. was finally removed, and two key executives, Shon Anderson and Matt Wolkow, stepped up to run the business effectively, given the lack of support they received up the chain. They implemented significant changes in the business, and it began making great strides in recovering. But the culture of the business was firmly entrenched and almost bullet-proof.

On the other side of the organizational divide was the Systems Integration (SI) business, which was more "fly by the seat of your pants" and reactionary due to the kneejerk characteristics of many of their customers. The projects were smaller than ES's, with short lead times and poorly defined scopes. Big projects caused SI fits, when brute force couldn't deal effectively with project problems. Yet when required to work with ES, they weren't interested in learning from them.

In 2010, our president laid down an edict that the two businesses would henceforth work together, sharing rather than duplicating resources and processes. This was a major cultural and process transformation, and it wasn't received well by either business. ES had a mature and disciplined organization, yet they were being forced to change processes to deal with an SI business they viewed as incompetent. SI resented ES arrogance, and they truly "didn't know what they didn't know." SI lacked project management processes to effectively support the ES business model.

After months of finger-pointing from both sides, we brought together the executives of the business units and threw down the gauntlet to try to push them to work together.

The businesses had to learn a joint business model, and we began by closing off the bad history and charting a model for success. The meetings were emotional, and I often felt like a referee in a slugfest. Reliving history and ripping scabs off old wounds didn't help, yet that happened over and over.

> The toughest octopi in the business world is organizational conflict.

While this went on for months, the businesses underperformed, and SE senior executives became increasingly frustrated with lack of progress. ES/SI leadership eventually stopped reliving history, learned to trust one another, and began to build a new operating model. I mediated the sessions, and if they failed to agree on an issue, I called them to the table and challenged them to make decisions. When they didn't, I did. And my decisions generally stuck, although I had no authority to dictate anything to anybody. I'd like to say this was a rewarding challenge over two-and-a-half years, but there was still much to be done when I retired. I guess I should feel good about the progress we made, but it wasn't the grand slam I wish it had been.

From Holding Company to Centralized Corporate Management

In 2007 I joined TAC, a building automation company within Schneider Electric (SE). SE's strategic planning was organized in three year programs, intended to provide employees and managers a clear understanding of the strategic direction of the company. The first program I was involved with was "ONE," intended to move the company from holding company to a partially integrated global corporation, simplifying the company under the SE brand, aligning many processes, and leveraging the size of the global company. Three years later, "CON-

NECT" was intended to continue the consolidation work started under "ONE." The company began consolidation of IT systems, aligned Purchasing, Materials, and Quality processes, and began consolidation of manufacturing operations, marketing, and administrative functions into centralized organizations. The concept had some merit, but the reality was really rocky.

Forced consolidation and centralization programs were heavy-handed and caused the operating organizations to focus inwardly instead of on the customer. Some of the initiatives had worthwhile goals, but the way things were implemented was problematic. French corporate groups responsible for the initiatives had little knowledge of our systems integration business, and they approached everything from a product mentality.

An objective of ONE was the deployment globally of SAP IT systems for all its businesses. SAP was a product-oriented system, awkward for almost everything else, and its support modules were not comparable to the industry leaders. I've never seen an IT installation project that finished on time, met its objectives, and delivered bug-free functionality, and when I last heard, SAP implementation had cost SE more than $500 million, been in work for more than six years, and was still only in limited deployment. Some of SAP's weaknesses were so problematic that new applications (e.g.: SalesForce.com) were brought in to replace inadequate SAP modules. The organizations responsible for deployment and support of the new systems became bureaucracies of the worst kind, dictating processes and policies with little knowledge of business needs.

Support functions that didn't support, corporate and country organizations that added overhead and little value, investment funding directed to French bureaucracies rather than customer-focused needs, and reporting mechanisms that were contrived rather than supportive—all these problems caused the businesses to take their eyes off their customers and expend energy dealing with bureaucracies. This aspect of my job—dealing with more than two dozen corporate mandates—was frustrating. There were a few successes; but they were insignificant compared to the organizational turmoil caused by the heavy-handed bureaucratic (and unfunded) mandates dropped on our heads.

Since I left SE in 2013, most of the American executives who built great American companies acquired by SE have been replaced by French executives. While I loved the people I worked with at TAC/SE, I feel nothing but

> Always challenge initiatives that do little to support your customers.

frustration for the rest of the SE world. I don't miss that part of my SE experience.

Money is earned at the pointy end of the stick, where company employees touch real customers. Corporate initiatives must be realistically assessed for the value they bring to customer-facing business units and customers. Assuming "one size fits all" in a diversified company is dangerous, and this applies to company executives, too. If they're not willing to engage with customers and add value through their relationships, then they'll likely just get in the way of the people who actually make money for the company.

Corporate bureaucracies, like political ones, often have objectives that do little to support the business units that actually earn money for the company.

Schneider Electric Global Quality Network

When I came to Schneider Electric in 2007, I joined TAC, a building automation company that was acquired by SE. TAC was a $3 billion global business with most of its sales coming from America and Europe. It was an energy management company delivering building automation and security products and solutions around the world. As a subsidiary of $18 billion SE, it was the only systems integration and projects business in SE's family.

SE formed a centralized Global Quality organization, and when it opened its doors, it housed more than thirty senior managers, all of whom felt compelled to dictate to the global business units how to conduct their businesses. TAC's President directed the company to establish a TAC Global Quality Network (GQN) in response to SE demands, but without adding headcount or cost.

Our first meeting was in Malmö, Sweden, TAC's global HQ, for the purpose of organizing TAC's GQN. The approach was to add zero cost and check the blocks versus SE demands. We began looking for common ground but floundered for three days, searching for a way forward. Once again, I stuck my nose into a leadership role, making suggestions to establish

> "Value-added" is sometimes hard to find in corporate organizations, which led me to organize as close to the customer as possible.

priorities and processes for managing quality globally. The group was willing to let me lead, although I already had a full-time job in the U.S. For the next nine months, we worked to organize TAC's quality processes and reporting systems to answer SE demands.

In the U.S., we had implemented a customer satisfaction (CSat) program based on the Net Promoter Score, and TAC's Executive Committee (ExCom) liked what we were doing. We were challenged to take the American system global, and I assumed responsibility for launching it through TAC's GQN.

A year later, SE launched an embryonic CSat program led by a manager whom I'll call Nigel—a British man with an insufferable ego and a conviction that he knew all there was to know about our business. He came in over the top, dictating how to handle CSat. Since we'd been running a successful CSat program for more than two years, we had good processes, but Nigel insisted on dictating changes. He called a meeting to review our CSat processes and whip us into line. We had spent an hour reviewing our processes when he demanded we change to his system. While a number of the changes were unproductive, others were actually counterproductive.

After trying to understand why we were being directed to do everything his way, I became frustrated and finally asked, "You don't care about our existing process and successful results, and you don't intend to do anything with the data we provide you. To change to your processes will cause us a lot of unnecessary work. Why should we change to do it the way you want?"

Nigel's response, *"Because I told you to!"*

After I picked my jaw up off the table, I said, "Hmm. Well, Nigel, I guess that's just not good enough."

This probably sounds like a recurring theme, but beware of corporate organizations that dictate rather than support, emphasize reporting over progress, and require you to comply with their dictates rather than support customers. Beware the ones that don't have customers as their focus.

Chapter Thirteen

Entrepreneurial Itch

Twice in my career, markets collapsed as part of a recession, and my companies were forced to re-structure. FSI International (1998) and ADC Telecommunications (2001) made major reductions to their executive groups, and in each case, I offered to leave the companies to support them as they dealt with downsizing. Following the second exit, my wife, Dottie, and I needed to make some decisions. At age fifty-one, I couldn't just quit working, so the question was what to do next? I was burned-out on corporate politics, and faced with the choice of looking again in the corporate world, or trying something on my own. We'd been blessed with great compensation over the years, and we'd built up our investment, IRA, and 401(k) accounts. Our retirement was in good shape, if we could bridge the gap from age fifty-one to sixty-six.

The opportunity to be my own boss won out, so I formed Stewart Consulting Company (clever name, don't you think?). I printed marketing materials and set out to be a consultant. I learned quickly that the hardest thing about owning your own business is business development, but as the word got out, I began receiving interest in my consulting work in the areas of corporate operations and strategic real estate.

Selling yourself is a constant challenge as you work on business development with companies who don't know you. Always research the companies you're targeting, and communicate your skillset emphasizing your value-added to each company. Tailor your approach, resume, and cover letter to emphasize your value, and be flexible as each meet-

> The hardest part of starting up any business is business development.

ing unfolds and you listen to the company's needs. Make yourself a part of their solution, as they describe their problems.

DISD Consulting Project

Soon after opening Stewart Consulting Company, I received a contract to perform a strategic real estate project for The Dallas Independent School District, inventorying DISD's administrative and support properties and recommending a long range plan for streamlining. My assignment didn't deal with school facilities, unless there was also an administrative or support facility on the site.

To understand the vision for DISD, I began with interviews of a long list of managers and department heads. While the number of DISD's students had remained relatively constant since the 1970s, the number of administrators had grown many times over. DISD owned twenty-nine administrative properties and thirty-nine vacant sites, and I documented the properties and put together recommendations to consolidate inefficient operations and sell unused properties. The project took three months for research and report preparation, and another six weeks for briefings.

I made presentations twice to the DISD Board of Trustees to provide my findings and recommendations, which were endorsed. Phase Two, developing detailed plans, was authorized, and I was asked to lead the effort. I was also designated to lead Phase Three, the execution phase. However, partway through Phase Two, my principal contact and advocate at DISD suddenly retired, and I wasn't comfortable with the new organization. I bowed out of the follow-on projects, turning leadership over to a large realtor. Ultimately, some of my recommendations were implemented, but the biggest single recommendation, dealing with the DISD headquarters building, has not been implemented and probably never will be. Working with a public entity is fraught with politics and sacred cows, and the pay is not very good. Be sure to clearly define the scope, deliverables, and acceptance criteria for your engagement, or you'll be continually pushed to do more for the same price.

> Being a consultant doesn't bring instant success. Be careful to manage the scope of your assignments carefully.

Mega Wraps

I suppose everyone at one time or another wants to own his/her own business. Mega Wraps was my time in that bucket (list). Don Creveling is a great friend who left his job as S.V.P. of Human Resources at JC Penney at the same time I left ADC Telecommunications. We had coffee one day and talked about how much fun it would be to work together. We both had good severance packages and enough finances to invest in a new business.

We decided to take a few months to see if there was something out there that might interest us, starting with a franchise broker who helped us identify candidates that we might like. After discussing several, we found Mega Wraps—a Toronto-based fast food restaurant chain with 100 stores—that was just entering the U.S. market. It was an upscale fast-food concept featuring pocket pita wrap sandwiches with healthy, fresh foods, and an upscale dining room. Its concept was what is called "fast fresh" today. The franchise chain was working well in Canada, according to all the information we received from HQ.

Don and I flew to Toronto twice to investigate Mega Wraps and meet with the founder and his team. We developed a business plan based on the *pro formas* the franchisor provided, but I was concerned from the first whether their restaurant designs could be built for the $125,000 they described. My estimate to build and outfit the stores was closer to $200,000, and in the end my number was accurate.

MENTORING INTENTIONAL EXCELLENCE

Mega Wraps' founder and President was a Jordanian entrepreneur, an interesting fellow with excellent promotional skills. He had minimal construction experience, and in coming to the U.S., he was opening a completely new market. We segmented a twenty-county region in the Dallas/Fort Worth area and prepared business models for various success rates. In addition to consulting our franchise broker, we engaged an investment advisor, and tried to pick the package apart. We all agreed that the concept was viable, so Don and I went to Toronto to negotiate our Master Franchise agreement. By the time we started our Mega Wraps business, in addition to more than 100 stores in Canada, Mega Wraps had sold territories in New England, California, Chicago, Colorado, Oklahoma, and Kansas.

Don and I came up with the start-up cash and formed a corporation to house the business. Our business plan included franchise sales, construction, and restaurant operations, and we prepared a UFOC (Uniform Franchise Operating Circular) for our Texas business. The pile of required paperwork for the small business loan we applied for was astounding. When we finally received it, we'd gone through a ninety-day wringer and *still* had to personally guarantee the loan. We'd have been better off if we had taken out a commercial loan.

From the beginning we recognized that neither of us knew anything about running a restaurant, and we needed someone to run our restaurants. One of Don's friends, Jerrell Denton, was an experienced restaurant and franchise manager with deep industry experience, so we brought him into our partnership as V.P. of Operations.

Jerrell and I attended a two week training course in Toronto, learning Mega Wraps operations, as well as the construction and franchising model. We would be operating restaurants, selling franchises, finding locations, constructing stores, and supporting franchisees, so we had a lot to learn. We negotiated a corporate deal with Sysco for supplying our restaurants, found a restaurant equipment distributor, and made a long-term deal for future restaurants. We were off and running!

We found a good site for our flagship store in a shopping center in Frisco, but construction costs became a problem immediately. When Mega Wraps Canadian HQ insisted we source all our millwork and furniture in Canada, the problems were amplified. Construction delays, signage disagreements, and unexpected sup-

> Make sure you fully understand the industry, market, and business models of any new venture.

plier problems conspired to chew up our bank loan, and more. Fighting our way through a myriad of difficulties, we finally completed our flagship store. When we finally opened, it was a beautiful store, but it was late and over-budget.

We were excited to open the flagship restaurant, which we used as a showplace for selling franchises. However, we immediately ran into trouble when HQ failed to meet promotional and operational support commitments, and when sales didn't achieve expected levels, we became concerned. We received no HQ marketing or advertising support, and food costs were well above HQ's *pro formas*. However, the biggest issue was the high rent in the Frisco area. Higher sales volumes would have solved that problem, but the combination of poor visibility, low margins, and lack of promotional support created a challenging financial situation. We did well when we sold catering orders, but there just weren't enough of those. We ran into cash problems within six months, and after eighteen months, we closed our Frisco flagship store and paid off all our creditors.

Our first franchise sale was to a retired sales manager and his wife, located at a busy corner half a mile from Plano Senior High School. The construction process went well, but the owners had visions of a beautiful, high-end store, and they requested upscale design features that inflated construction costs. They hired too many employees from the beginning before getting their feet on the ground, and while we gave them extensive help and waived royalties and advertising fees for a time, in the end the store went under. I was heartbroken because I thought it had a great chance to be successful. When the restaurant closed and the owners declared bankruptcy, we were left with $56,000 of his unrecoverable debt.

Our second franchise sale was to two former technology executives. It, too, was unsuccessful, but for a completely different reason.

> Rosy sales and cost projections don't help. Be realistic, and don't add overhead and staff until the business demands it.

The store went into a high rise office building on the north side of downtown Dallas, where we negotiated an outstanding rent-free lease, and designed an efficient restaurant. Mega Wraps HQ insisted we use one of their corporate partners for construction, and we gave the contract to the Wichita builder. He and two employees came to Dallas for the project, and when the company ran out of money, instead of paying suppliers and subcontractors, the principal took our money and left town. One day he just disappeared, leaving his employees stranded in Dallas with unpaid motel bills and wages. He refused to take phone calls, taking our money and leaving us with a pile of mad employees and subcontractors. I made arrangements with his employees to continue the project, but I had to pay back wages and living expenses. We could have sued the principal and filed charges, but we would have had to hire an attorney, and we weren't going to recover our money from him in any case. Equipment suppliers and subcontractors filed liens against the project, and I visited every contractor to renegotiate their deals. By the end of the project, we paid more than $50,000 of duplicate expenses, but we paid every debt.

When the restaurant opened, it started with great sales, and we were pleased with the prospect of having a profitable store that paid its bills and royalties. We helped hire and train a great young restaurant manager who was energized to sell catering, in addition to presenting an excellent image to his professional clientele. But, when I returned from a trip to HQ, I found the owners had cut their own throats. Without consulting us, the owners fired our manager and installed a brother-in-law as manager, because he needed a job. He was the exact opposite of the first manager. He had just been released from prison, presented a poor image, had terrible customer skills and no restaurant experience, nor had he been trained. He stole the owners blind and completely alienated his customer base. Sales declined to almost zero, and the store was in trouble from the day the new manager walked in the door.

> The success of your business depends on those people you hire, train, and equip to deal with your customers.

One day, the owners walked out and locked the door, taking the keys. By the time we were able to get inside and figure out what had happened, the equipment, furniture, and inventory had been foreclosed, and restaurant employees were left demanding back wages. The franchisees disappeared, refused to take phone calls, and left us with thousands of dollars in unpaid royalties.

Now down three stores, **we had one more chance.** We were approached by Southern Methodist University about putting a Mega Wraps store at their Plano site. They offered free rent and utilities, which made it an excellent, low-overhead deal. We were able to use equipment and furniture from our closed Frisco flagship store, and Jerrell operated the store with three employees. The SMU store started strongly, and when we sold catering orders for conferences, we did very well. But, when we had to depend on walk-in business, we were barely able to keep our heads above water, though we remained open.

I've never worked so hard in my life, especially when we had large catering orders. We started at 4:00 a.m. cooking breakfasts for large groups, then transitioned immediately to preparing lunches and hosting breaks. Often, I went to Sam's Club and filled my truck, inside and out, with food and supplies for large orders. Loading and unloading was torture, and running carts back and forth across the SMU campus to manage catering was exhausting. (Remember my proclamation when I was twenty that I didn't want to do manual labor?)

The end of our SMU venture came when Jerrell, who was operating the store, received an offer from a barbeque restaurant chain to become V.P. of Development. He couldn't turn it down, nor could we ask him to, and we had no way forward. I informed the SMU Site Manager that we would be shutting down, and a group of friends helped pack and move everything to a storage location. I began paying off creditors, and we made the decision we would not declare bankruptcy.

> Don't fool yourself into thinking success is just around the corner if you can't see it. Make fact-based decisions.

I attempted to contact the President at Mega Wraps Corporate HQ, to inform him we were shutting down and to try to collect some of the money he owed us. That was when I learned that he had walked away from the business, leaving an office full of employees without pay, and his franchisees holding bags full of empty promises. If HQ had assets worth going after, we would have prevailed in a lawsuit, but we would have had to hire a Canadian attorney and get in line behind Mega Wraps' Canadian creditors. Last I heard, the founder was back in the Middle East, doing who knows what.

I compiled a daunting list of outstanding obligations, began selling off equipment and furnishings, and negotiated with our creditors to settle our debts honorably. Don Creveling is a great man, and an even better friend; he stayed with me to the bitter end, and we paid our debts until we had finished the Mega Wraps business completely. We loaded a trailer with our remaining furniture and equipment and drove to a liquidation center, where I sold the trailer load for a few hundred bucks. We paid off our debts as soon as possible, and the business finally closed in 2007.

What I Learned A number of lessons came from my Mega Wraps venture. But first, I want to say a giant thank you to my wife Dottie, who gave me 100 percent support throughout my hair-brained venture. Even when things got bad, and I was waking up at 3:00 a.m. to try to fix unfixable problems, she supported and loved me through it.

I also want to say a huge thank you to Don Creveling, my partner and long-time friend who stood with me to the end. He joined me in making payments to the last penny of our debt, and he never complained. He is the true definition of a friend, and I feel blessed to know him.

In assessing the failure of this entrepreneurial business, there are a lot of places fingers could be pointed, but in the end, it only matters how you finished, not why you failed (unless I'm planning to try the restaurant business again … *which I'm not!*). Here are some observations on our business venture … I hope it doesn't come across too much like finger pointing.

> Maxing out a credit card is a terrible way to raise cash for your business!

Business development is the hardest part of any business. Branding your business, finding customers, and generating demand for your products are difficult. While there are people who are willing to put everything they have at stake, that wasn't me. If you make the leap to own your own business, be sure you have funds to support and potentially close down the business. Even after the doors close, you will have obligations that won't go away. And lenders are in business to make money, demanding personal guarantees, and they will come after your personal assets to pay off your corporate debt.

When setting up your business, I recommend putting it in a corporation to protect you personally from the liabilities of the business. Make sure you set up separate bank accounts and don't co-mingle assets or funds. If for some reason you have to defend the business in court, or claim bankruptcy, you must be able to demonstrate that assets, liabilities, and funds were handled separately. Be sure to observe all legal requirements for filings, board meetings, and management of the business, and keep meticulous records with a solid paper trail to prevent opponents from penetrating "the corporate veil."

Don't make the mistake of paying yourself, adding overhead, employees, or non-essentials until the business is profitable and clearly ready to absorb the additional cost. Don't give customers deep discounts or take on investors under severe terms just to pull in a few dollars of sales or operating cash. Don't fool yourself into thinking success is just around the corner if you can't see it and know what has to happen for it to become real. Dogged determination, hard work, and refusal to fail can be outstanding traits, but when applied to an unsuccessful business, they can be deadly. When the business is unlikely to succeed, requiring another infusion of capital, it may be time to close the doors. Don't delay the decision when hope is your only ally. It will only make the situation worse and burn up cash that you will need to shut the business down.

> "Never, never give up" sounds good, but there are times when cutting your losses is the best decision.

When you close a business, take the actions that your values tell you are right. Pay your debts rather than walking away. Creditors will often accept reduced amounts if you tell the truth and ask for the smallest amount they would be willing to accept. They'll appreciate that you're handling your business honorably, and you'll be able to sleep well at night.

My Mega Wraps venture was stimulating and frustrating, exciting and exhausting, terrifying and satisfying, challenging and rewarding, a source of pride and regret, a sense of independence and a humbling feeling of inadequacy, a commitment I couldn't walk away from, and a responsibility to others that was daunting.

Chapter Fourteen

Finishing Well Intentionally

J ust as intentional beginnings are important, getting off on the right foot and recognizing what it takes to be successful, so are honorable endings. Finishing well has always been one of my priorities, whether it's finishing a project, a business assignment, or a job. Never burn bridges, no matter how satisfying it might be to vent your emotions. I've left several jobs in my career, and I can honestly say each time I landed on my feet in a better situation. Chapter Nineteen spells out my philosophy and process for responding to the loss of a job. I recommend you use it as a "check list" for moving to a better position.

Finishing well also pertains to how you pass your legacy along to the next generation. Late in your career, your thoughts will turn to giving back, which is very fulfilling. Don't lose the opportunity to express yourself honestly to the next generation.

The Going Away Party

What follows would be, I hope, impossible in today's corporate world. For me, it was terribly embarrassing, and it violated my moral standards badly. Good-humored recognition is one thing, but out-of-bounds behavior is unacceptable. It was a less than "delicate ending," and I didn't enjoy it a bit. It's a lesson in the wrong way to finish.

In 1989, when it was announced that I was leaving Texas Instruments' Defense Business for a new assignment within TI, the Lewisville team threw a goodbye party for me. More than 150 people attended, and it was certainly memorable. The atmosphere was congenial, the goodbyes were heartfelt, and I enjoyed being nostalgic with so many friends. Everything was going well until I saw a young lady enter the room. I didn't recognize her, but she was quite attractive, and I noticed she was carrying a boom box. The crowd receded to the edges of the dance floor, leaving me exposed, and my alarm bells started going off. The young lady (I'll call her Shelly) brought a chair to the middle of the dance floor and set her boom box under it. The room became quiet as Shelly walked in my direction, beckoning with her finger for me to come to the middle of the dance floor and have a seat. I looked for cover, but everyone had pulled back, and I had no way out. I knew this wasn't going to go well, but I walked to the chair, acting braver than I felt, and Shelly sat me down. She turned on her boom box, and as the music played, she began dancing and taking off her clothes. She offered me the opportunity to help her strip, which I declined. I sat in the chair, hands on my knees and looking straight ahead, which only challenged Shelly further. As she disrobed, three scallop shells came into view, two located on her upper body, and the third was hung strategically below her navel by rawhide thongs. Maybe if I'd given her a response that acknowledged her work, she would have stopped. But I didn't, and she didn't. I stared straight ahead, looking over her head at the far wall, and she took that as a challenge.

As Shelly escalated the situation, she tried a number of sexually-explicit actions designed to gain a reaction from me. I had no clue what to do at this point, so I kept my eyes fixed on the far wall, and my hands latched to the seat of my chair. I was badly embarrassed, and Shelly eventually gave up and paraded around the dance floor, minus the top shells, and receiving an appreciative round of applause. When she left my vicinity, I exited to the edge of the dance floor and hid behind a group of friends. She danced around, one shell short of complete nudity, then eventually packed up and left. At that point, the party lost steam, but that wasn't the end of the story.

Several folks approached to tell me how sorry they were that I was treated that way, and I went home and immediately told Dottie what had happened. I was completely embarrassed to have to tell her what my friends had done to me. I suppose they were entertained, but I wasn't.

Two weeks later, an anonymous package arrived at my new office, and I opened it to find a large package of photos from the party. While most of the photos were keepers—pictures of friends and colleagues telling me good-bye—the others were of Shelly and me. They were incredibly graphic, and it was immaterial that my eyes were focused on the far wall. I immediately destroyed the photos and told Dottie about them. She already knew about the party, so she understood the situation when the pictures showed up, but I'm constantly haunted by the thought that somewhere out there is a set of film negatives of that whole sordid affair.

> You have more control than you think over bad situations.

In retrospect, I should have asserted my "authority" over the situation. I should have stood up for my values more strongly, and set an example for others. I don't know if this type of behavior exists in today's workplace, but I haven't seen it in the past two decades, so maybe the corporate world is cleaning-up its act. In case there's any confusion, I suggest you always set appropriate limits for the behavior of your organization. While you can't control what others may choose to do, at least you can make your expectations clear. And don't compromise your integrity when put in uncomfortable situations.

High Visibility Firing

After Texas Instruments' MAS business I was managing took the severe financial hit from a Detroit auto company, we suffered a year of decimated profitability that the business never recovered from, and we made the decision to shut down MAS. While we didn't leave any customers hanging, we stopped marketing the business, and began moving MAS employees to other positions within TI.

Gary Slagel was the general manager of the MAS business. He was a senior TI manager, and he was also the long-time mayor of the City of Richardson, where TI's headquarters are located. Gary was a great ambassador for TI to the community, and when we made the decision to shut down MAS, he engaged as a true professional and did a great job of carrying out a very painful decision for his business. He successfully placed almost all of his people in other jobs at TI, and his plan for shutting down the business was implemented. In the end, though, we were unsuccessful at finding him anything else, and I had to lay Gary off. He was a professional about that, too, and after leaving TI he went on to be an entrepreneur and start-up coach. Gary would probably say that being laid off by TI was a positive for him in the long-run, but it wasn't pleasant. To my knowledge, he never said a negative word about me or TI, and I learned a great deal about professionalism from Gary. I have great respect for him, but I still carry the distinction of laying off the mayor of our city.

> The only way to handle difficult employee situations is to show respect, honesty, compassion, and open communications.

First Career Failure

After leaving Texas Instrument's Defense Business, I went into a global leadership role leading a 500-person IT organization. I was an experiment, bringing an Operations manager into an IT role, trying to change the culture to be more customer-focused. In this case, "customer" was defined as the money-making businesses of TI, its customer-facing organizations. As I look back on my experience in the Information Technology Group, there wasn't a time when I felt comfortable. ITG's executive group was constantly on edge, and there was more political posturing than at any time in my career. I don't think ITG management ever trusted me, and my immediate boss was adept at playing corporate politics and deflecting responsibility. He was forced to accept me in an attempt to inject real-world experience and the voice of the customer into the insulated IT organization, and it never sat well with him. My biggest challenge was that I had no IT credibility with my employees, and my commitment to customer support wasn't matched by my new organization or bosses.

By 1992, after two years, it became clear I wouldn't be successful in turning around the IT organization. Bill Mitchell and my mentor, Jim Houlditch, who had sent me to ITG with a "money-back guarantee," had left TI in those two years, so I was hung out with no sponsors. My Defense peers

> Sometimes it's risky to be the first person to try out a new company model.

helped me with kind words after the fact, admitting that from the start they didn't think I had a chance to succeed for a number of reasons outside my control. One of my peers was direct when he said he felt badly for me, since, "You were given a bag of s***, and when your support left, you were really screwed."

To this day, I still have some bitterness about this situation, and I thought about taking the issue up the chain to make an appeal. But I chose not to for a number of reasons. Handling failure with grace is hard, but it always pays to take the high road. Saying what comes immediately to mind may be emotionally satisfying, but it only invites the other party to respond in kind. Escalation of the situation is not beneficial unless you're sure you're on solid ground and know where to find support.

Give your loyalty to your company, but always know there may be people who don't have your best interests at heart. Becoming a sacrificial lamb can be a real possibility, and while handling failure with grace is hard, it always pays to take the high road.

Losing a Job After Twenty-One Years

A year later, with the termination of TI's relationship with Turbochef, it was the end of the road for me at Texas Instruments. I had a discussion with my boss about next assignments, and it was clear he had nothing for me. I visited with several Defense executives and friends, but with both of my sponsors gone and the defense industry shrinking rapidly, there was no future there, either. Trying to force TI to make a spot for me would have been counter-productive, and any job I landed would likely have had little growth potential. Besides, forcing a problem is not the best way to deal with your company, potentially alienating your executive group at a time you need support.

> When you see the end coming, consider taking the initiative.

When I suggested that perhaps I should move on, my boss appreciated and supported my suggestion, and sent me to the V.P. of HR to negotiate a severance package.

It had been more than two decades since I had been without a job, and I had a time of initial panic. James Jackson was an old friend, dedicated to the company but sad to see the situation I was in. It was obvious that he was embarrassed he had to lay me off. Taking a lesson from Gary Slagel's professional response a year earlier when I had to let him go, I decided to be professional and maintain a positive attitude. I went in with a low-key, non-confrontational approach, which proved helpful as we designed the severance package. James stuck his neck out for me on several points, and my response helped improve the severance package. It actually turned out to be a lucrative separation.

While scary at the time, it became a positive career move. Could I have tried to force TI to make a new position for me? Maybe, but that would have created hard feelings, and looking back at it twenty-three years later, I was much more successful leaving TI than I would have been if I had stayed.

My two decades at TI were filled with non-stop promotions and new challenges, the most interesting years of my career. One of the factors for my success had been the feeling of belonging and support from TI's executive team, which gave me the freedom and confidence to lead boldly over the years. I felt someone always "had my back," and when asked to go a new direction, I was the good soldier.

So, my latest situation felt unreal, and I went through a strange mixture of emotions, routinely ambushed by feelings I'd never experienced before. I felt abandoned, ashamed I couldn't fix the problems of the past two years, fear for the future, feelings of letting down my family and my company, regret, disillusionment, and even relief that the uncertainty was over. I wish I could have done something to make everything right again, as it had been when I was in the Defense business, but those times were over and there was no going back.

In the end, I felt I was thrown away unceremoniously and without recognition, after twenty-one years of sixty-plus-hour weeks. I didn't even get a goodbye party this time, but it was time to move on.

When out of viable options, working cooperatively with your employer gives you the opportunity to improve your exit terms and severance package. Never burn bridges. When you lose a job, you must choose one of two responses: either view the loss as a tragedy and a time of fear, or as a new opportunity. Those who choose the latter are more able to take control of their lives and approach their careers as something they actively manage, rather than having a job at the mercy of others.

Keeping Your Chin Up

Now let's fast-forward to 1998, when my new company, FSI International, suffered a severe downturn, and the company had to downsize. I was E.V.P. of Global Operations at the time, and my boss offered me an executive position in Europe, but I declined and decided to negotiate a severance agreement to exit the company. Leaving FSI was hard, since I had rebuilt the Operations team and helped the company achieve aggressive goals. And I had made a number of good friends there. I scheduled a goodbye speech for my management team, and I was nervous in front of more than 100 great folks that I'd led to substantial success. I wanted to say thank you and goodbye in a classy way, and I was concerned about being "emotionally ambushed," since I'd never been able to talk coherently when emotional.

I told my team that my job at FSI was complete, and I was leaving the company. I said I was extremely proud of the team we'd built, and I felt they would be successful at whatever they tackled in the future. I told them I supported the changes being made to transition FSI to a smaller, more efficient company, and asked everyone to

> Saying you're an architect of the new organization rather than a victim is so much better.

be a part of the solution. I exited the room before I got too emotional, since I'd invested a lot of myself in the folks in that room, and leaving those special people was the hardest part of my departure. Later I was asked why I didn't come back; my team had given me a standing ovation. I wish I had gone back, but I didn't, and I can't change that now. I appreciate the gesture, and I remember fondly the team we built and the successes we enjoyed at FSI.

Moving on with class is important to me. As I've said, never burn bridges, and leave on your terms. You never know when you may need help from someone you knew in a former lifetime, nor when you might want a good reference.

Telecom Collapse

A few months later, I joined ADC Telecommunications as the V.P. of Corporate Operations. The company was growing organically at rates above thirty percent, and acquisitions put ADC's total growth rate above fifty percent during the telecom bubble of 1998-2000. It was a great time, with bonuses and incentives paying off hugely. At the Board meeting in October 2000, the Board approved an aggressive 2001 plan with huge sales and profit growth. Almost insane, except that the prior two years had demonstrated the Telecom Equipment market was highly lucrative, and ADC was deeply embedded in the growth of the industry.

Three months later, when the Telecom industry's downturn became a meltdown, ADC was vulnerable, and the business plan of October 2000 became a derelict. In January 2001, the Board met again and approved a revised 2001 plan which reflected—instead of significant sales and profit growth—a contraction of almost thirty percent. Really, really ugly. I was amazed at the speed of the reversal.

Shortly thereafter, the Board decided to change leadership, and a new President, CEO, and Chairman was hired. He held interviews with the executive team to address the deteriorating financial situation, and he released many of the executive team and reduced corporate staff dramatically. When he called me in, we talked about future roles and responsibilities, and I'm sure he had already made up his mind to let me go. By this time, we had moved back to Texas, and I received another good severance package. A few weeks later, I made a goodbye trip to Minnesota to wrap up loose ends, and when I visited some peers, I received some startling comments. Since I was no longer a threat to anyone, I received some honest (dismissive) comments from those who fought me so hard while I was at ADC. The CFO was a real surprise, making an arrogant comment that I think reflected his personality when he said, "I figured it was only a matter of time. I knew you never had a chance."

There's never a reason to be condescending or dismissive when someone is headed out the door. Burning bridges, for any reason, is in bad taste and can come back to haunt you in the future. Sometimes a job comes to an end for no other reason than a change of command. Other times a leader is hired but is not positioned for success. You should assess any position with that in mind, and if you decide it's something you want to do despite the risks, go ahead.

The prior CEO took an enormous buy-out with him, and the new CEO didn't stay long, cashing in on the lucrative separation clause in his contract. The CFO became the new CEO, and mercilessly "hatcheted" the company, dressing ADC for sale. While I admit to leaving ADC with a bad taste in my mouth, my time at ADC was worthwhile, if for no other reason than the company-paid relocation back home.

My three years at ADC went by quickly, and the role was one of the most instructive of my career. Political back-stabbing, organizational resistance, dismissive treatment, hostility, and other disagreeable behaviors seemed to be much more the norm at ADC, and I can't say I enjoyed my stay there.

> Sometimes a job doesn't work out for no reason other than a change of command.

By the time I left, we were delivering savings of more than $50 million per year, and though I found a number of people who welcomed my help, too many others had other motivations. The compensation was great, and the company-paid move back home was a bonus, but my primary takeaway was to do a better job of watching my back.

Lincoln County Networking Group

In 2001, good friend Dick Ivey and I met and realized we were both in the same boat. We'd both been executives in the Telecom Industry when it melted down, and we left in search of our next challenges. We began meeting weekly for coffee and networking, and at some point, we began welcoming others who were in the same boat. Before we knew it, we were having coffee with a dozen people per week. We unearthed and shared job leads from our networks, and invited recruiters to provide us with search requirements. Our numbers grew quickly, and we decided to organize the group formally. Since we were meeting at a local restaurant called the Lincoln County Grill, we chose Lincoln County Networking Group for our name, and we built a website to publish and archive job leads and networking materials. Our growth accelerated from twenty members to more than 100, and we began inviting speakers for our weekly meetings. We made a conscious decision to be independent, with zero cost, and the price of membership was the willingness to help others.

Before long, LCNG grew too large for the small cafe, and we were asked to leave. We kept the name, though, and fifteen years later, we're still the Lincoln County Networking Group. Dick is our fearless leader, I'm still the highly-paid (all of *zero* dollars!) secretary, and good friend Eric Sluder is the technical whiz who manages our website. Af-ter losing our meeting place, we found another location on the Southern Methodist University campus in Plano, where LCNG

> Combine your strength with others. You never know where and how you'll grow.

meets to this day. At its peak, LCNG had more than 4,000 members na-tionwide, and we distributed more than 5,000 job leads per year. During the 2001-2004 recession, more than 100 job seekers attended our weekly meetings, and the networking and job assistance was a heavy load. Today, LCNG's attendance is down to a small group that meets weekly, but we still have 1,400 on-line members, and I administer several hundred job leads per month.

I'd love to know how many people we've helped over the years. As with most non-profits, though, you can't fully appreciate the impact you have on people; you can only be faithful to serve. While the hours spent managing LCNG haven't been financially productive, the satisfaction that comes from helping others is highly fulfilling. I recommend becom-ing involved in a charitable or service organization that helps people. Giving back is a responsibility for those of us who have received help from others and been successful.

Retirement from Schneider Electric

When I joined TAC in 2007, it was with the intention of working for three years, to age fifty-nine. By 2010, I had assumed responsibil-ity for Operational Excellence, and we had built a high-performance organization of thirty employees. I enjoyed the work and especially the autonomy and credibility I had with the executive team. Our initiatives were having an impact on the business, so I stayed an additional three years.

Mentoring Intentional Excellence

In January 2012, I visited my three bosses and told them of my plan to retire a year later. I wanted to transition gracefully, with plenty of time to bring a successor on-line. They appreciated my direct approach and agreed with my recommendations for succession. Jeff Smith was the logical successor, and when we met to discuss my plans to introduce him to the "Wayne Stewart Fire Hose Training System," he agreed enthusiastically. He stepped up to the plate over the next year and responded extremely well to the new role.

> Once you decide that the end of your career is in sight, I hope you have the opportunity to retire on your terms and potentially have the largest impact of your career.

Mid-way through the transition process, I was asked by my S.V.P. to take a leadership role with the single objective of profit improvement. Jeff accelerated his move into his new role, while I was still available to support him. I was given broad authority to challenge the company's "seat of the pants" project management culture, identify needed disciplines, tools, and training to turn the ship. We made solid progress, and when I left SE in early 2013, Jeff was fully "in the saddle," with a strong set of plans for improving the operations of the company.

During my six years at TAC/SE, I feel best about building a high performance team that drove operational improvements and supported customers. I loved the people I worked with and enjoyed challenging the business to change its ways of doing business. Mentoring senior executives was enjoyable, and being that senior advisor (*pain in the butt!*) that every executive wants was rewarding. I also enjoyed having an impact on younger managers, the next generation of leaders at SE. There is nothing more enjoyable than helping bright, energetic, talented, and motivated managers succeed.

Late-career roles can become your most rewarding. Once you decide that the end of your career is in sight, I hope you have the opportunity to retire on your terms and potentially have the largest impact of your career. Mentoring, advising, special assignments, and enabling others are immensely satisfying roles, a fitting way to end your career. For those who have trouble turning loose, it will require you to turn the reins over to others, allowing them to stretch themselves to continue your legacy.

An Exit Speech. . . But Not Mine

A good friend, Jon Majors, gave me a lesson in management. He is a retired Marine, Facilities Manager for a large educational institution. He made the decision to leave for a better opportunity, and what follows is Jon's exit speech to his organization, packaged in an email. With his permission, I'm including it here. Jon talks about servant leadership, and I've taken it to heart and recommend it to you.

Wayne,

Yes, I'm going to a great opportunity. Better security, pay, pension, insurance, etc. XXXXXX is not an inherently bad company, but there is, after two years, still a lack of direction, clear vision, and strong leadership. It breaks my heart to leave my team here without a servant to lead them. I spoke with them this morning and challenged them with the following:

If I have led you well, demand the same from whoever takes my place, and hold him or her accountable for what I did right and ensure they do not repeat my failures. Basically, I am giving you permission to talk behind my back.

My vision two years ago for this team was to be a team of up and coming managers. A team of men and women who own their jobs with the courage to fail and the drive to succeed. You are that team and I thank you for making a vision realized.

We have praised, coached, and held each other accountable. We had some that didn't make it on our team, and they had to go because we had a mission to do and a vision to realize. In all of that you have been nothing but professional.

I have tried to "lead up" and prime the pump for true leadership, but I think, no, I know, that those efforts are over. I do see some good coming for the XXXXXX team here, but it is going to be very painful and not something I am willing to be a part of anymore.

I wish you all the best. Jon

Unfortunately, it's a message that leaves Jon's team without their leader. I'm sure they felt hurt and abandoned, but Jon left them with a roadmap for success in whatever organization they found themselves. Jon's focus was on the excellence of his team and their contributions to the success of his organization—great qualities. Jon is a Marine, and I know it hurt him to leave his troops, but he's a good man, and all of us are better for knowing him.

Part Two: The Lessons

The absence of learning is the beginning of failure.

Chapter Fifteen

Where Your Career Takes You

Where I Learned

With a working career spanning fifty years, I won't bore you with a résumé, but the progression sets the stage for what follows. Entering my professional career at Texas Instruments in 1973 at twenty-two, I was instantly supervisor of eight senior employees supporting a large Defense manufacturing project. After adding projects and supervisory responsibilities, my first management role in 1977 was Manufacturing Engineering Manager for a $30 million Defense program. At thirty, I was promoted to Division Operations Manager, running manufacturing operations for a $200 million multi-project business. At thirty-three, I assumed responsibility for a much larger Operations organization, building a $100 million, 5,000 person Defense manufacturing operation supporting a $1 billion division. At thirty-nine, I moved to TI's Information Technology business, managing a 500-person global IT organization and a $50+ million automation and software products business.

In 1994, leaving TI after twenty-one years was hard, but it was a time of learning. At forty-four, I entered the executive world at FSI International in Minnesota, succeeding to Executive VP of Global Operations. Following the acquisition of an English subsidiary, I launched into the world of corporate and international governance as Board Member for the English company. In 1998, I moved to ADC Telecommunications as VP of Corporate Operations, and was fortunate to move back home to Texas before the telecommunications industry meltdown in 2001.

Beginning in 2001 and continuing today, I scratched my entrepreneurial itch and went into business for myself. I've opened consulting, ranching, and restaurant construction/franchising businesses. In 2005, I joined the Board of a Washington, DC-based building automation and security systems business, where I was elected Chairman in 2006. A year later, I was invited to return to the corporate world at the parent company, Schneider Electric, an $18 billion global energy management business. Completing my corporate career in 2013, I retired from SE as V.P. of Operations for its Americas Building Automation business. Since then, I've written two books, opened a publishing business, served on corporate and charitable boards, and today I operate a family ranch and do some writing.

So, there it is in a nutshell: a career of learning.

How I Learned

Whether learning from our own successes and mistakes, or from observing others, continual learning offers us the opportunity for continual improvement. Change—the necessity of career growth—occurs as lessons are learned, successes are emulated, and failures are assessed and rectified. Behavioral change requires hard work to commit to, and to demonstrate, the change on a consistent basis. Changing the expectations of others takes time; they must recognize that we've changed and develop confidence that our behavior will consistently reflect that change.

Failure to learn and change can be the result of laziness or complacency, believing that what's brought us success so far will carry us successfully forward in the future. It leads to stagnancy of thought and behavior, and it risks mediocrity and failure in a competitive world.

Ego can bankrupt performance quicker that almost anything, accruing to overconfidence and a sense of invincibility that sinks our boat as soon as someone has a better idea or a more-winning way. Ego's opposite is humility, required to seek learning intentionally and commit to change. It can be perceived as weakness in the cut-throat business world, but being a servant-leader demands this trait, and those who "seek first to serve" are

> The best kind of behavioral change is intentional and disruptive.

consistently more successful in leading others.

But learning is only part of the process, and its benefits are only realized when it causes change. The best kind of behavioral change is intentional and disruptive. Changed behavior, coupled with the intentional pursuit of excellence, is the stuff of career recognition and growth.

Those who embrace career learning, the pursuit of excellence, and intentional behavioral change will be greatly in demand in the business world. Welcoming change is a winning trait in managers and executives, and those who have read to the end of this book will gain insight into the exciting (and sometimes painful) world of success in the business world.

My nose was bloodied on multiple occasions as I learned management lessons, not the least of which dealt with corporate politics. As I moved "up the ladder," I learned from the world of executive leadership, entrepreneurship, and corporate boards. At the end, I found my most satisfying role as an executive who was senior advisor, corporate leader, and mentor to presidents.

Recognizing the Need to Change

Early in my career, I discovered that not only did I not have all the answers, but in many cases I didn't even have the right questions. I realized I was in a "sink or swim" situation without a life preserver, and the only path to success demanded that I learn from everyone. Approaching issues with a humble spirit and willingness to learn from others—no matter their station—was rewarding. Much of my success is attributable to adopting the observed traits of others who were successful in difficult environments.

Making *intentional and conscious changes* in my management style was necessary several times, and some were significant enough to require me to intentionally change my personality. Pushing myself to adopt traits I wasn't comfortable with affected both my professional and personal lives. Perhaps the most important was the recognition early-on that success (survival) would require me to abandon my naturally-introverted, "back seat" personality for the more-successful traits of straightforward and transparent decision-making, self-starting leadership, and assertive personal interactions. In a harsh operating environment, allowing others to run over me would result in loss of respect and relegation to the world of "low achievers." I tried always to recognize and hold fast to my values, despite pressure to take shortcuts. Developing "backbone" in my personality was one of the hardest things I've ever done. I had to move from the back row to a leadership position, taking risks and being recognized for succeeding more often than failing.

> Allowing others to run over you results in loss of respect and relegation to the world of "low achievers."

The Intentional Career

A typical career progresses through phases that depend on the quality of the lessons learned and intentional changes that are on-going. Developing the ability to learn and put into practice the resulting changes is part of the maturing process, continuing unstopped even beyond the end of your career. Career phases are a progression of building blocks, beginning with the bedrock of your life—your core values—and progressing to the pinnacle, the Sharing Phase. Each phase is characterized by lessons learned, progress, maturing, and changes, demonstrating who you've become. The *intentional career* looks something like this diagram below.

SHARING	TEACH	*WHAT YOU DO WITH IT*	LEAD TEACH MENTOR PASS IT ALONG LEARN
LEADERSHIP	DELIVER	*WHO YOU BECOME*	LEADER EXECUTIVE FAMILY LEARNER
GROWTH	LEARN	*HOW YOU WORK*	EXECUTION TEAMWORK SKILLS ADOPTION COMMUNICATION LEARNING
ABILITIES	PREPARE	*WHAT YOU BRING*	SKILLS TALENTS EDUCATION PERSONALITY WORK ETHIC LEARNING
VALUES	DEFINE	*WHO YOU ARE*	FAITH ETHICS FIDELITY LEARNING

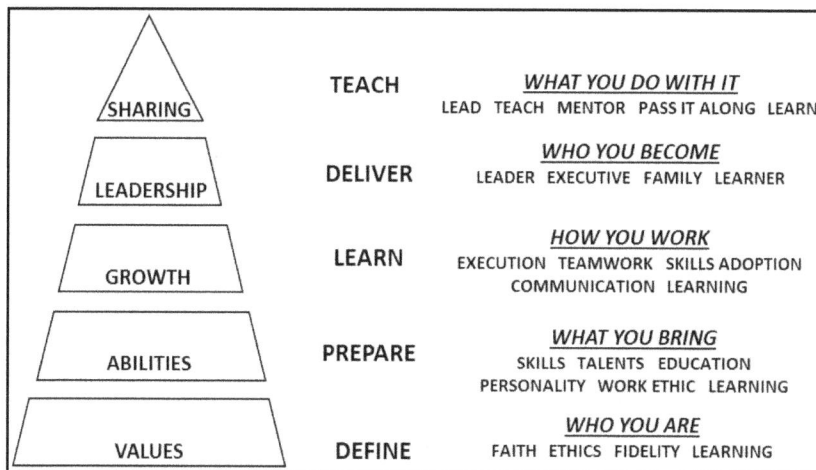

Phase	*What Happens*	*Your Identity*	*Elements*
Values	*Define*	Who You Are	Faith, Ethics, Fidelity
Abilities	*Prepare*	What You Bring	Skills, Talents, Education, Personality, Work Ethic
Growth	*Learn*	How You Work	Execution, Teamwork, Skills Adoption, Communication
Leadership	*Deliver*	Who You Become	Leader, Manager, Executive, Family
Sharing	*Teach*	What You Do With It	Leader, Teacher, Mentor, Pass It Along

Core Values

You are defined by your core values, more than you'll ever realize. They are an obvious part of your personality, and people recognize and respond to them, even when you think no one is watching. Over time, they comprise your character. Some values are defined before you enter the work force, instilled by parents and teachers. Others are adopted or confirmed as you are successful when you depend on your core values to lead you. Adoption of, and commitment to, the core values of faith, family, country, ethics, and fidelity, are the most critical set of decisions you'll ever make. Your values are confirmed as you are successful with critical decisions, and once committed to, you trust and strive never to violate them.

> Define the bedrock standards in your life and don't violate them: faith, ethics, integrity, fidelity, reliability, and quality.

Violations of your core values always come with a cost, and most come back to haunt you.

Faith has been instrumental in my life and in the success of my career. Many years ago, a wise mentor helped me gain clarity in my life's priorities, both personal and professional. As he talked, something in me resonated, and he helped me redefine my priorities. I wasn't always this way, and I've sometimes disappointed myself, but I'd like to think I held to my values and priorities pretty well. Throughout my life, my integrity has grown as my faith has grown.

A good friend challenged me to pour more of myself into this book than I had originally intended, sharing the development of my faith and its role in my professional life. It's a bit hard for me to be so open and vulnerable, since I worked largely in agnostic, technical businesses that had little room for anything but work. I hope you see the role my faith and core values have played, and perhaps it will be an encouragement for you.

Abilities

Your abilities come from diverse sources: God-given talents, developed skills, education, training, learning, experiences, and intentional changes. They include physical and mental aptitudes: work ethic, willingness to take risks, endurance and physical abilities, and scientific and artistic talents.

> Abilities are granted and grown, gifted and developed.

Training and learning equip you for your career, and when your abilities are set on the bedrock of your core values, they represent the foundation for your career and life.

Growth

Growth is the career stage when the application of your core values and abilities toward goals sharpens your skills, enables successes, builds your reputation, and begins your career ascendancy. Your work is a constantly-changing mix of individual assignments and teamwork, leadership and following direction, adopting and sharpening skills, and building communication and interpersonal abilities. This is the time when learnings and their resulting intentional changes are most important in giving your life direction. Even so, at times you will make trial and error decisions, not convinced of your direction, and you will learn. On the other hand, using the counsel of others you respect and trust, when combined with your learning and experiences, successes will build your credibility as a successful decision-maker and leader. Successes at this stage propel you to the next phase, where all that has gone before has prepared you to lead others using your acquired wisdom and people skills.

> Growth occurs when you apply your core values and abilities toward goals and you experience success (or failure).

Leadership

Whether early or late in life, to succeed in a career you must learn to lead: teams, work groups, disparate company and customer organizations, and senior managers. As a leader, manager, and executive, you must depend on others to carry out your vision. Human

> Processes are managed; people are led.

193

relationships can be difficult, either greasing the skids of progress or consuming you with the minutiae of constant problems. If you're to lead successfully, you must also learn from those you're leading, recognizing that the combined brainpower and skills of a team are far more effective than your own abilities.

Sharing

The last stage of your career will be defined by leadership and "sharing." For many, it's the time when they've achieved the goals of their professional lives, and can "take their foot off the achievement gas pedal." I didn't say they quit working hard, but their objectives change. Others never quit the treadmill of career striving, but in either case, it can be the

> Part of your legacy allows others to remember and respect you for what you taught them.

most rewarding phase of your career. You're working for the joy and satisfaction of this stage, recognizing the abilities, achievements, and potentials of others. Perhaps you'll be finishing preparations for retirement, applying your skills to charitable or public service missions, or leading large organizations. But your motivation will shift from climbing corporate or entrepreneurial ladders to gaining satisfaction from enabling and helping others succeed. Even then, your lifetime habits continue, especially the enduring curiosity of learning new things and improving as a person. Whether manager, executive, mentor, writer, advisor, teacher, or leader by example, this phase bestows on others the wisdom and lessons of your lifetime. It's a part of your legacy that allows others to remember and respect you for what you taught them. Living-out your values throughout your career and into the "Sharing" phase gives you a satisfaction that your life has mattered.

You will notice that I have not once mentioned age. That's because people pursue careers at different rates, with different levels of commitment, subject to variations in their willingness to learn, change, and let others teach.

Work/Life Balance

How do you balance your career with your personal and family commitments? We've all seen people who sacrifice everything for their careers, then spend the rest of their lives with regrets. I'm not in the "worst offenders" category, but I do have regrets for being on the road so much, and spending so much time at work. While it

> Your work/life balance should be a personal and intentional decision, made with your family.

paid off financially, providing a comfortable lifestyle and gaining career recognition, we could have gotten by on less. For my TI career, I *averaged* more than sixty-five hours per week. I know, because I kept records. The unwritten policy was that you worked dawn to dusk on weekdays and a half-day on Saturdays. During crunch times, the demands were heavier, and traveling on company business was a burden. Over the course of my career, I flew more than 3 million miles, mostly at the back of the bus, and the separation from my home and family came at a cost. After leaving TI, I reduced the frequency of family interruptions, but by then both our kids were mostly grown. Suggestion: If you're struggling with this issue, create a log of hours "on duty" versus family time. You may be surprised by what you see.

Your work/life balance is a personal decision, and the hours of hard work early in your career are an investment in your family's future. On the other side, once lost, special family times cannot be recovered. One of my bosses, Jack Swindle, told me, "I've known too many people who didn't have time for their families, but they had to make time for a divorce." The key is balance. For those coming after me, I suggest making an overt decision for yourself and your family to define your priorities, whatever you decide them to be.

Be a Master Negotiator

In negotiations, culture will be a major factor. Always know what you'll be dealing with when you enter a negotiation. For instance, within the U. S. government, there are three types of customers: elected officials, bureaucrats, and "warfighters." Their motivations are different, and you need to be able to recognize and deal with them. Elected officials' priorities are the need to be re-elected and accumulate power. Bureaucrats' top priorities are to preserve the bureaucracy and look good in the transaction. "Warfighters" are those whose top priority is to better serve their country. When you deal with each of those groups, recognizing their priorities and helping them to satisfy those needs will generally help you get a better settlement.

Negotiating tactics can vary hugely. In Asia, a deal is never complete, even after hands are shaken and contracts are signed. You'll often be badgered and threatened for more concessions, sometimes when you're trying to make delivery of your products. In the Middle East, negotiations can be dramas of the highest order, and feigned insult is often practiced ("the flinch"). Negotiating in the construction industry can often include high-decibel, profane arguments and intimidation. On the other hand, charitable organizations often use "soft hands" negotiations, with nuanced arguments and appeals for "the good of the children."

Do not, however, interpret the above to imply I'm suggesting you compromise your integrity just because the norm in the other country would make the decision or action acceptable. In the 1980s, TI was negotiating a contract with the Greek government, and a Greek citizen (not employed by the government) indicated he could act as our agent and "grease the skids." In today's parlance, he would be a "fixer." At the time, we chose not to pay him for his services, and we got the contract without his grease. It was perfectly acceptable in Greece at the time, but how would it look in the U.S.?

These kinds of decisions can often be difficult, and besides the legality question, you must examine the services offered versus the amount being requested, to evaluate the equivalency of the transaction. Here in the U.S. lobbying is a lawful business, attempting to influence government decisions, policies, and laws to the benefit of an industry or constituency. But there are strict laws that come into play, and more than a few people have gotten themselves into hot water

> How would it look if your decision were to be headlined in your local newspaper?

by walking the boundaries of, or crossing over, the limits of the laws. When faced with a hard decision in any area, my advice is the following; it's a simple test of the effects of your decision. Consider how would you feel if your decision were to be headlined in your local newspaper? Not just its legality, but its moral intent and consequences? I recommend always taking the high road.

Let Quality Be Your Watchword

Any discussion of quality must begin with your ethical standards: faith, ethics, integrity, fidelity, reliability, and quality. These are your bedrock, and they're all indelibly linked. Conduct yourself with integrity, refusing to deal in areas of questionable ethics, and if you have to make an unpopular decision, as long as it's based on your ethical standards, it's hard for the boss to override you.

The quality of an organization is closely aligned with the integrity of the people within it. Quality is a way of life, not a product feature. During my years at TI in the 1970s and 1980s, we were constantly in search of a magic "token" that would instantly create high-quality products and processes. Unfortunately, then—and now—no such token exists, and any attempt at a quick-fix is doomed to fail. We spent decades adopting and refining quality processes and programs, most of which we embraced prior to their general recognition across industry. Juran, Krensky, Willoughby, Deming, SPC, SQC, TQC, JIT, Zero Defects, Effectiveness Teams, Quality Circles, Lean, Malcolm Baldrige National

> Ethics and quality are your bedrock, indelibly linked.

Quality Award, and others were adopted and contributed to Texas Instruments' quality culture. Ultimately, TI built its own quality system, an amalgamation of initiatives that resulted in a culture of excellence that continues today.

Blunt Talk and Your Intentional Career

Now it's time to talk about what it takes to be a senior executive. My life and career followed a path that valued, to the best of my ability, ethics, people, and honest management as the key to managerial success. Unfortunately, there are companies that value results above all else, sometimes at the expense of quality and integrity. You see them on the front page of your newspapers far too often. I've worked for men who have gone on to huge corporate success after mortgaging their core values. In some companies, that's what it takes to be ultimately successful.

I intentionally chose not to follow that path. It cost me, I'm sure, because I tried to take the high road, even when it meant taking responsibility for problems and failures that others may have deflected or denied. I suppose I was at times viewed unfavorably, as Dean Clubb once said to someone else, "You've cinched your chastity belt up so tight you're choking to death."

You need to make a conscious decision for your career. Will you honor your core values, or will you compromise them to climb the ladder. It's not necessarily either/or, as there are wonderful examples of companies that honor outstanding values, to the extent of refusing business that comes with an ethical cost. But there are others that put so much emphasis on results that the methods to achieve them are insignificant. Make your decision, and hold to it. People are watching.

Chapter Sixteen

Mentoring the Next Generation

Over forty years of gaining experience and observing others have helped me identify a number of winning traits that I adopted for my management style, and I found some that didn't win. On the positive side, a humble spirit is critical if you want to win the hearts and minds of your people. There are certainly examples of arrogant, heavy-handed managers who have succeeded, but they leave a wake, and they don't often achieve the potential of their people. If you want to unleash the potential of your employees, you need to be willing to learn from them.

The most difficult part of any professional's job is building and maintaining positive relationships with co-workers, subordinates, and bosses. Managing employees adds another layer of challenge to the equation, and the secret is to provide your folks transparency, integrity, humor, the example of hard work, compassion, consistency, and proactive communications.

Consensus-building is an effective trait, the ability to bring involved-parties into the decision-making process and gaining common agreement for proceeding forward. Done well, there's no ambiguity about direction and commitment, since everyone had a part in the decisions. But becoming dependent on consensus as the only decision-making process is a mistake, since it's typically time-consuming and can allow strong personalities to diffuse the entire process. If achievable in a reasonable time frame, by all means use consensus decision-making for your team. But when out of time, or when consensus is not going to be reasonably achievable, you need to be prepared to make accurate and decisive judgments in stressful situations.

Over fifty years, I've had to deal with bad situations, some of which you've read in this book, but for the vast majority of my career I've had the good fortune of great relationships. I count as good friends so many of those with whom I've worked, and I look forward to staying in touch and continuing to enjoy those relationships. What follows is a collection of observations and suggestions for maximizing the effectiveness of your career. While somewhat random in their arrangement, they are instructive at all phases of your career.

Executive Strengths and Weaknesses

When asked to describe the traits of successful executives, I like to use contrasting examples of two Schneider Electric executives. **Bill** was a dynamic, charismatic, salesman-turned-Executive V.P. He was a good friend, and I enjoyed working with him, but he was so energetic and undisciplined that he confused the organization. Everyone loved him, and he had a brilliant knowledge of the industry. He was a good strategist, had a wonderful sense of humor and great leadership style, but he also had some flaws. Bill's verbal communications were sometimes unclear, with a style that sometimes left us guessing. His brain ran faster than his mouth, and at times Bill could be indecisive and inconsistent, giving different direction on the same subject in different meetings. I sat through meetings where issues were clearly defined, everyone had a say in the needed direction, yet no decision was made. Rather than providing direction, Bill left the issue on the table and adjourned without making a decision. Hence, organizational confusion.

Jerry was also charismatic, but he came from an operations background, stronger at giving direction and making clear, consistent decisions. He had a great personality, was a wonderful leader and communicator, and he was dynamic and challenging. But his weakness was that he wasn't strategic. He had it in his head, but when it came time to communicate his vision, he left something to be desired. He was excellent at making decisions and giving organizational direction, but without clearly articulated strategic direction, too many decisions had to come to him. With clearer vision and strategic direction, his team could have made good decisions on their own rather than waiting for Jerry to decide. If you have trouble communicating your vi-

> Never be afraid to hire the best talent you can find, complementing your weaknesses and building the strongest possible team.

sion, your people will struggle to "catch it." They have trouble carrying out your vision if they don't understand it.

Bill and Jerry were both strong, charismatic leaders, but one was not an effective executive. Bill lost momentum by waiting for the organization to make decisions. Even then, some of his managers, sensing Bill's indecision, didn't support them, and he was indecisive in taking action to hold his people accountable. Jerry, on the other hand, was crisper in reaching decisions and holding people accountable, but his vision wasn't clearly communicated. The key for success for both executives was to recognize their weaknesses and complement themselves with good people around them who were capable of compensating for their weaknesses. Jerry was able to do that, but Bill never made that step.

Managing a Large Organization

In the late 1980s, the Texas Instruments Operations organization I had the privilege of leading was large and complex, spanning six sites with more than 5,000 employees, and supporting a nearly-$1 billion business. Most of the employees were manufacturing workers, although there were also a large number of engineers, purchasing, and administrative folks. The keys to effectively managing an organization of that size were to set clear objectives and expectations, communicate openly and honestly, and hold managers accountable. Openness, genuineness, integrity, clarity, and objectivity all play a part in reassuring your people that they will have a fair hearing. Even if they don't get the outcome they want, they're treated fairly and told in a straightforward manner why a decision was made.

I often had to make hard decisions, and I wasn't always good at communicating bad news effectively. There were times when I knew I had a difficult confrontation coming up, and I sometimes procrastinated, which generally just made the situation worse. I would fret and worry, taking problems home with me, when what I should have done was take the initiative in raising the issue, trying to defuse the confrontation and settle it amicably. Even when delivering bad news, take the honest, transparent approach. Don't beat around the bush and don't try to deflect blame when you're at fault. Go in with the confidence to calmly state the situation, and try to have a recovery plan already underway.

> Even when delivering bad news, take an honest, transparent, and timely approach.

On the other hand, in forty years of managing and supporting multi-billion dollar businesses, supervising people and managing organizations large and small, I never went to court for any reason. That includes business relationships and employee relations. Of course, there were problems and disputes, but I always gave the parties a fair and open hearing, understanding both sides of the issues, and I knew enough law to be clear on the points that were lynchpin. It's not about always winning; it's about ethically managing your business.

Humor and Fun, Powerful Management Traits

Over the years, as my management style evolved, I became more aware of the benefits of using humor in running my operations. Dean Clubb, Texas Instruments' S.V.P. and my boss for six years, taught me more than anyone else about how to use humor with your people, your peers, and especially your adversaries. He had a way

> Humor is the antidote to stress.

of disarming problems with a down-home, country sense of humor expressed even in the most difficult situations with a smile and a pleasant retort. I've given you samples of Dean's clever humor in the chapter "Dealing With Big Personalities." In the same chapter I described Allen Thomas's witticisms. But don't confuse the two. Dean's humor was real and disarming. Allen's was intense, deprecating, and intended to carry a forceful and unpleasant message.

Humor is the antidote to stress. When used effectively, it disarms high-stress situations and brings the discussion back within manageable bounds. It doesn't surrender an argument, but it lets everyone know that anger and shouting are not necessary to come to an agreement. The opposite, what I call the "New Jersey Construction" attitude, is filled with shouting, obscenities, and threats, and while I suppose there are those who feel anger and confrontation are the ways to manage a business, I don't. It took me too long to come to this conclusion.

Likewise, having fun at work is an outstanding trait of managers that build highly successful teams. The enjoyment of working together and building strong, positive relationships holds your group together even when issues arise and pressures build. Most people will be more receptive to whatever you have to say if you are able to put them at ease first with humor. And having one another's back is a great way to ensure your customers get your best efforts and support.

Whether in the work place or after hours, being able to enjoy being together as a leadership group builds teamwork. Leading with a caring, humorous, and committed style builds the confidence of your team members and encourages them to take risks and work hard for the best interests of their team. Later in my career, I enjoyed hosting fellow workers at my ranch for weekend hunting trips. The relationships developed there have been long-lasting and deep, with the honesty and transparency that encourages the letting-down of guards and establishing an equality that allows you to relate more effectively on a "human" level. I strongly encourage you to look for opportunities to enjoy your work and your people, through both a humorous personal style, with an objective of making fun a part of your team.

Managing Effectively In a Chaotic Environment

There were often times in my career when I felt overwhelmed. I tend to be overly-detailed, and my family made fun of me for anally-planning our vacations (I'm better now). On the other hand, I was always a multi-tasker, so I could feel confused as to what to tackle first. Here's my advice: while it's tempting to grease the squeaky wheel (responding first to whoever yells the loudest), you have to decide the correct priorities given all that's on your plate at a given time. I always prioritized customer issues, keeping them front of mind until they were resolved.

At my desk, I always tried to accomplish what was immediately before me before moving on to other things. That meant I tried to deal thoroughly with an issue (ex: an email) before moving on to others. In earlier days, I read a piece of advice that said, "Don't touch a piece of paper more than once." In today's world, that includes, "Deal with emails only once before moving on." Further, when dealing with a problem requiring coordination and a number of steps, always push the ball forward as far as possible before moving on to another subject. Two things happen at that point: first, you get the satisfaction of knowing you've done everything you can at a given time, and second, you've taken the initiative. I've told you before the benefits of leading rather than following, and in this case it's really true.

> When you're a multi-tasker, you'll need to use discipline in defining priorities and accomplishing work. Hint: customers come first!

While sometimes being accused of being a *"Ready, Fire, Aim!"* manager, it was part of my philosophy of trying always to lead rather than follow. The risk is that you might make a mistake with a hasty decision, but I always found that the benefits outweighed the risks.

Management Style Evolution

I started my career at Texas Instruments, and it could be a brutal work environment at times. Many old-school managers had a lot of "beat down" in their management style. I tried to have a more encouraging and inclusive management style, although I found myself going into "dictator" mode at times, especially when that was the expectation of those above me. I tried to eliminate the harshness, promote inclusiveness, and "spread the wealth" when it came to successes. This came at a time when the old line of TI executives was moving on and a new breed was ascending to TI's executive levels. The old school could be harsh, fostering unhealthy competition and a survival-of-the-fittest mentality. The new style was more inclusive and instructive, challenging rather than demanding, encouraging versus punitive, cooperative rather than combative, and that was the style I wanted for myself. In the "sink or swim" culture, I learned that "clenched-fist" management can obtain short-term results, but over the long term, it engenders fear and a "play it safe" mentality that doesn't bring out the best in people. Employees can be good soldiers, but it's neither a good training ground for future leaders, nor for achieving organizational potential.

I'm now part of the "old guard" and perhaps viewed by others as too much old school. But I feel strongly that management styles that value people and their individual abilities are always superior to being demanding and overly-directive. Over forty years, my management style evolved, reflecting my work environment, learnings, and intentional changes. While it sounds good to say your management style is consistent and everyone is treated the same, that's just not true. My style changed over the years, and at the end, I called it scalable, which really means flexible based on conditions. Over my career, I went from:

- *Hard-nosed management* to
- *Participative management* to
- *Collaborative management* to
- *Scalable management.*

The **Hard-nosed management** style was the way I started because that was what was expected of me in the early years. Most of my bosses weren't intentionally mean or condescending, but they issued orders that they expected would be carried out. It took me a while to realize a better way. A hard-nosed management style doesn't go well with someone who actively learns from his people, so I suppose I was always more "human" than "hard-nosed."

Participative management was most useful when I began managing folks. I learned early on that asking for suggestions was a good way to draw your people in and give them a sense of ownership in the decisions. I was still directing too many activities personally, but when a good idea came from someone else, I was comfortable letting the person run with it.

Collaborative management came along toward the middle of my career, helping me engage my entire team in solving problems and managing projects. Slower, but when you can afford the time to reach consensus, it's a successful approach with today's workforce.

Scalable management means using a management style that is effective for a situation. I prefer a collaborative approach that gives everyone a voice in major decisions. But if consensus doesn't develop in a reasonable amount of time, you should ensure everyone has a chance to state his/her position, then you need to make a decision. You should always temper the desire for consensus with the need for speed.

> Teams and committees are not responsible—people are.

Risk-taking is a desirable trait that is not regularly fostered in clenched-fist management and consensus styles, so I learned quickly that, after decisions were made and it was time to execute the plan, you have to ensure that one person is responsible for leading, making decisions, communicating, and accountability.

Teams and committees are not responsible—people are. Responsibility and authority should always be vested in a single person, so there's no confusion. That person must be challenged and empowered to aggressively push forward, leading fearlessly.

Leading *Versus* Following

One constant throughout my career was that my management style was virtually always about leading rather than following. When you're leading, you set the agenda and everyone else must react to you, as you focus constantly on the customer. You push the envelope for speed, cost, quality, and service. It's riskier when you're leading, but as long as mistakes are

> When you're leading, you set the agenda and everyone else must react to you, as you focus constantly on the customer.

dealt with honestly and openly, they can be corrected. I expected my employees to make mistakes on occasion, and when they happened as part of advancing a priority, anything that broke along the way could be fixed. As the old adage says, "If you're not the lead dog in a dog sled trace, the view is always the same."

An old adage from my TI days is still true today. While it references the personality of engineers who constantly tinker with their designs, creating a moving product-design target, it's also applicable to many other scenarios. Author unknown, it says, "There comes a time in the life of every project when you shoot the engineers and go into production."

Today's workforce, composed of Baby Boomers, Gen Xers and Yers, Millenials, and whatever-comes-next-ers, is more complex than ever, with priorities and motivations that can vary widely. Learn all you can about the cultural traits of each generation, learn from the people with whom you work, learn from those who lead you, and learn from those who make mistakes and/or succeed; then, adapt and improve.

Chapter Seventeen

The Management Punch List

Managing Your Boss

Throughout *Mentoring Intentional Excellence* I've discussed how to succeed in whatever role you're working. In addition to dealing with people transparently and with integrity, there's another skill that will support and encourage your success. You need to learn how to manage your boss(es) and the management chain.

Start by recognizing their priorities, skills, and strengths/weaknesses. Be sure to support them in their weaknesses, volunteering overt support when you know they are struggling. Make sure your communications are proactive, keeping them informed and never allowing your management chain to be blindsided. When giving a "heads-up" on a problem, be sure to describe your actions already underway to resolve it.

> Never give raw data to an executive.

When you push for an initiative or an unpopular position, couch your argument in terms of data and the value proposition ... what it means to the organization. Financial justification often removes emotion from the debate. However, it's risky to use too much data, because you run the risk of getting buried in the details.

My rule of thumb is the higher you go in the organization the less pure data you provide. At each successively-higher level, move farther away from data and emphasize analysis, conclusions, and actions to ad-

Communicating With Management

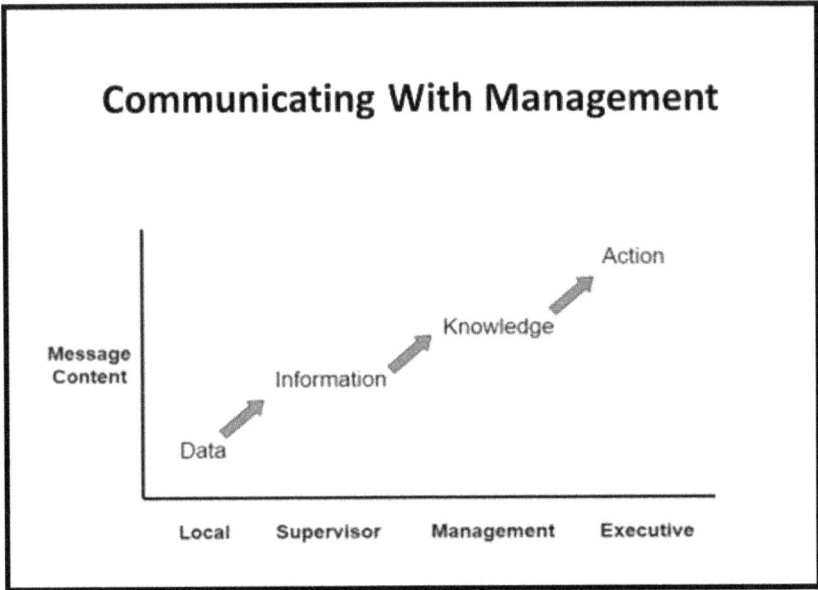

dress the problems. Never give a pile of data to executives, since the outcome will be either their boredom, or loss of control as they digs into it.

It's important in dealing effectively with others (bosses included) to recognize and effectively manage expectations, both yours and theirs. Making rosy commitments can be high risk unless you're confident of the outcomes. I've seen sales managers who intentionally kept a war chest of "in the bag" orders in their desk drawers to ensure they didn't miss their forecasts. I'm not suggesting unethical treatment of financial results; rather I suggest you couch your commitments to include a realistic assessment of the risks and potential outcomes.

There's an unpleasant subject in this area that deserves discussion … whether you are able to trust your boss. I've had good bosses that I would trust with my children, and I've had bosses that I felt uncomfortable trusting, but on one occasion, I had a boss who was an absolute snake. We had major

> When you can't trust your boss, make sure you're documented to the hilt.

disagreements when I called him on some of his behaviors, and I had to leave the organization to escape him. If you find yourself in a bad situation with your boss, I suggest you find an ally, mentor, or HR person up the chain whom you keep informed of your situation. And be sure you are documented to the hilt with his inappropriate behavior.

Fixing Problems

All of us are called on to fix problems, and the hard ones, especially those with technical content, can become extremely frustrating when a "shotgun" approach doesn't result in resolution. Difficult problems require a disciplined approach to find permanent resolution. There are many books and courses on

> The first step in problem resolution is to stop the bleeding.

this subject, so I won't go too deep with my discussion. Instead, I'll give you some practical guidelines for approaching major problem resolution, especially when you're responsible. I found it helpful to use a simple three-step process to set the stage for successful resolution, with minimum damage.

1. **Stop the Bleeding**—Halt whatever process is generating bad results. Don't continue producing defective products or unprofitable outcomes.
2. **Fix the Problem**—Identify and resolve the root cause of the problem. Otherwise you're treating symptoms and the problem will continue. Restart and test the corrected process.
3. **Clean Up the Mess**—Deal with the carnage left by the bad process. And be sure to close all the communication loops.

There's a corollary to the above when you're dealing with personnel issues. Any time you are presented with a dispute or employee behavior problem, remember that there are always two sides to any issue. Consciously seek out both sides of the problem before acting. And for major issues, consult your support professionals (HR, Security, Legal, etc.)

before making a final decision. Document your meetings with affected employees, and after making a decision, close the issue with a "memo to file" that defines the problem, approach, findings, involved parties, and decisions. Retain the file in case you have to defend your decision at some future point.

Productive Meetings

I've been in far too many meetings that floundered their way through unproductive, unfocused, and ineffective (or no) agendas. In the end, the results were hard to find. So, to help you sharpen your "meeting skills," what follows is my process for organizing and delivering productive meetings, especially those that address a particular problem.

> Meetings should always have a purpose, agenda, and understanding of what constitutes success.

- Respect everyone's time, starting and ending on time.
- Open the meeting with a clear description of the meeting's purpose and what will comprise a successful outcome.
- Present the issue and look for consensus within the stakeholder group as to root cause and needed actions. Do the actions treat symptoms or root causes?
- If consensus is not available in a reasonable timeframe, move to a more direct management style. After stakeholders have their say, make a decision for the group and give everyone in the room a "now or never" opportunity to register a complaint. Appoint a team and leader, and send the team off to execute the decision.
- If there is lack of agreement or success after the above steps have been taken, move to a more-strongly directive mode. Give direction and hold each person accountable for his/her role in

implementing corrective action. Caution: when you do this, you become the de facto team leader.

- If commitment problems still haven't been resolved, be prepared to use a more-direct approach, giving direction, tracking progress, and taking overt action if someone doesn't support the direction. This may mean removing someone or taking action to defeat his opposition.

- Close the meeting *on time* with confirmation the meeting met its success factors.

Chapter Eighteen

The Stewart Theory of Change Management

OK, I'm old school. Why can't people just do what they're told? (Yes, I'm joking) The task of corporate culture change (turning a large ship while it's underway) has taken on greater significance in recent decades as employee expectations, work environments, and management styles have evolved. In the old days, change occurred when the boss ordered his managers to implement a change. In turn, they ordered their managers to do the same, and the orders rolled downhill and were followed. As Baby Boomers gave way to Gen X and Y, who were better educated and expected to know why they should behave in a certain way, iron-fisted executives found that giving orders wasn't as effective as it used to be. Making organizational change demanded a new model. The term "change management" came to mainstream businesses as it was grudgingly accepted, gaining momentum as successes were recognized. As employees became smarter and more independent, and organizations became more virtual, gaining commitment and redirecting organizational inertia became imperative. Change management became a recognized term for process change, and expertise in changing cultures became important.

I admit to being a dinosaur. I always favor action, feeling more comfortable leading than following. Making organizational change happen became a problem for me when I joined ADC as V.P. of Corporate Operations. As the executive of a support organization, I was dependent on persuasion to make changes, rather than giving direction and

having it followed. Emphasizing value propositions (financial
justification), many managers
followed my recommendations
using common sense. In a similar role at SE, I found managers

> Change management can turn into an endless pursuit of herding cats if you're not careful.

who didn't care about common sense; they were more concerned with protecting their turf than working for the common good.

In today's business world, there are good troops who do what they're told, those who like to lead, those who need to be persuaded, those who respond to value propositions, those who are reluctant to change, and those who refuse to change. The following is a tongue-in-cheek summary of my approach to change management in a large organization. While humorous, there's truth in it, and I recommend moving through these steps with specific intent, and an eye on the clock.

The Stewart Theory of Change Management
Sequentially Deployed

Step	Action	Who
1	Lead Some	Early Adopters
2	Push Some	Open Minded
3	Bribe Some	Value Proposition-motivated
4	Drag Some	Late Adopters
5	Threaten Some	Resistors
6	Nuke The Rest	Permafrost

Remote Operations

I've always been concerned with the risks of "work from home" programs, and despite their popularity today, I still think I'm right. Many of today's employees work remotely, showing up at the office occasionally, insulated from the inconveniences of commuting to a company facility. Their perspective is that they're more efficient working from home, but I don't believe it, primarily because the times I've worked from home, I've felt inefficient and constantly interrupted. The informality of working from home, in a sometimes "sloppy" environment, can also cause a lack of discipline in many people.

Setting the efficiency question aside, I think there are risks to this style of work that make it less effective. Here are some problems I've recognized in *managing* remote employees, as well as some of the risks of *being* a remote employee.

- Inefficiencies—the potential for interruptions and loss of efficiency.
- Loss of community and teamwork—if you're not face-to-face with co-workers, subordinates, and superiors, how can you truly be on the "same sheet of music?"
- Difficulty assessing employees' performance—how can you assess their effectiveness if you don't see them in action?
- Slow communications and alignment, with difficulty reading visual communication clues.
- Frustration due to isolation, without having access to others to vent and commiserate.
- Difficulty building your reputation—if you're not visible to superiors, they have trouble knowing you and your capabilities.
- Coffee/vending machine conversations—informal interactions in random meetings, when you discuss issues and actions in a non-threatening setting.

- Loss of "boss-time"—losing informal interaction with peers, mentors, and bosses.
- Ambiguity in your team without the ability to walk into an office and close the door.

I could go on for some time on this subject, because I feel strongly about it. Remote management has both personal and managerial risk, and if forced to work remotely, ensure that employees commit significant time to travel for face-to-face team interaction.

> **Personal interaction is always preferable to remote operations and electronic communications.**

What's On Top?

While writing this book, I was asked to include the top five lessons learned of my almost-fifty-year career, and what follows is my list. Here's where I recommend you hang your hat.

First, *establish and hold to your values*, the same values for both your personal and professional lives, inseparable. Your business associates need to know what to expect from you, and living your life according to your core values defines your character.

Second, *learn intentionally everywhere*. Observe, listen, lead, take risks, own the outcomes, and make intentional improvements.

Third, *value people above work*. When your people have personal crises, let them know that their families and personal health come before their jobs. Help them through the difficulties. At the end of your career, your satisfaction will come from the people you help.

Fourth, *be transparent*. Communicate with honesty, realism, and openness, and always be approachable.

Fifth and finally, *have fun*. Working is so much more enjoyable when you're not a driven grouch. Don't come to the end of your career remembering only negatives.

Chapter Nineteen

Losing Your Job—Transition Philosophy

I exited three companies in my career with nice severance packages, which wasn't accidental. This goes to the heart of my transition philosophy. Anyone who loses a job has to choose one of two responses: either view the loss as a tragedy, or an opportunity. Those who choose the latter are more able to take control of their lives and approach their careers as something they actively manage, rather than having a job at the mercy of others.

When it became evident that my roles would substantively change, I chose to take control of the discussions. Since the situation isn't pleasant for the person on the other side of the table, providing a suggestion that addresses the company's concerns, while setting the stage to your advantage, you're starting from a position of strength. Be realistic; don't try to force a poor situation to continue. If you insist on arguing about losing your job, complaining about mistreatment, or otherwise venting, you'll waste time and potentially alienate others. If the company is struggling to find a job commensurate with your abilities and pay, they'll be relieved if you suggest an exit plan.

Be unemotional; these situations are rarely surprises, and you can usually see something on the horizon and prepare. Companies have severance policies, but they also have flexibility. If their policy is for six months of severance pay, and that's fixed, you can improve the situation by working on other valuable factors, such as delaying your severance date, payment for outplacement support, travel and relocation reimbursement, extended benefits, accelerated vesting of stock options or retirement accounts, etc. Work with HR until you get the basics on the table, then visit

> When you lose your job, you can choose to be a victim … or a victor.

with your executive to see if you can move the package even more favorably. Every time I transitioned, I landed my next job before my severance pay ran out, and we were able to bank some cash. It's all about attitude.

Be positive, realistic, cooperative, and unemotional and you will have a much better chance of coming out on the positive side of any job transition. Here's my recipe for making an effective job transition, once the loss of your job appears likely.

First, *be realistic in assessing the situation*, and recognize it as an opportunity for career improvement. Be unemotional in all discussions, and *never burn bridges!* Get over the emotional baggage as soon as possible. Move through the anger and grieving emotions quickly, recognizing they are normal. Don't dwell on negatives.

Hit the ground running. Don't take six months off until your severance money is gone. While it can be comforting to sit at home and surf the job boards looking for your next job, that's a low-probability approach. Instead, network, network, network. Contact recruiters boldly and make yourself available to them as both a resource and a candidate. Reach out to your network, and maintain detailed notes on your contacts and referrals to *their* networks.

Don't get discouraged. The more senior the position you're seeking, the longer it can take to find your next job. According to an old rule of thumb, finding a new job can take a month for each $10,000 of salary. Today, that might be updated to a month per $20,000 due to inflation, but, in any case, mine never took that long. I was always aggressive in going after my next opportunity.

When going to a networking meeting, be prepared. *Every networking meeting or introduction is an opportunity just waiting to be unearthed.* Do your homework on the company and person you're meeting, custom-

> Anyone who loses a job chooses one of two responses: view the loss as a tragedy, or an opportunity.

izing your resume. Focus your elevator speech (your thirty second presentation of yourself, your capabilities, and your objectives), and your responses to the questions you know you'll be asked.

Be confident and honest. No matter the circumstances of your departure from your prior position, you must be positive about your next one. You have a lot to offer, and your attitude should reflect a positive outlook and energy. No one wants to hire someone who acts defeated. Don't blow smoke; be realistic and aware of the interviewer's priorities. Even negative responses should be viewed as opportunities to learn. When you enter someone's office, try to relax the tension and establish common ground. Take a look at personal memorabilia in the office, pick an item that looks interesting or reflects a shared interest, and ask about it. Show some personality and a sense of humor.

Never tell the interviewer your salary expectations. Respond with something like, "My prior base salary was roughly $xxx, plus bonuses and stock options, but I'm flexible based on the opportunity. I'm sure we can work out the financials once we define our mutual interest."

At the end of the day, finding your next position is the most important work you have to do, and you'll be most successful when you make a full-time job of it.

Wrapping It Up

As we bring this book to a close, I want to ask you for something. If you've read to this point, please send me an email (wayne@sgrpublishing.com) and let me know your thoughts. If it's been of benefit, I'd like to hear that. If you found it to be irrelevant, please help me improve it. But most of all, let me know how you're doing. I can't help myself; I enjoy mentoring and helping others!

Best wishes for your career. May it be always intentional.

If you are interested in having a Mentoring Session with me, have me as a Keynote Speaker, or a seminar on one of several subjects, please contact me at wayne@sgrpublishing.com.

About The Author

J. Wayne Stewart is a native Texan, and a graduate of the University of Texas. He married Dottie Coke in 1973, the same year he began his professional career at Texas Instruments. After twenty-one years at TI, rising through the ranks leading large Defense Operations, he moved on to Operations Executive positions with FSI International and ADC Telecommunications. Following the Telecom meltdown of 2001, he went out on his own, opening consulting, restaurant franchising, and ranching businesses. One of the consulting assignments resulted in being invited back into the corporate world where he finished his career at Schneider Electric.

After retiring in 2013, Wayne took up writing and ranching full-time, and he recently opened a publishing business to handle publication and distribution of his books, *Yesteryear, The Next Generation* and *Mentoring Intentional Excellence.* Two more books are in the works, *Passing The Torch*, a faith-based book on the transition of generations, and *Generations of Texas*, a history of eight generations of Texans, from the Texas Revolution through multiple wars and into the twenty-first century. His website also offers his father's *Yesteryear*, a compilation of Jeff

About The Author

Stewart's popular newspaper columns about a way of life that no longer exists. West Texas in the Depression, Pearl Harbor and WWII, and the executive world of the 1900s, these are all part of Jeff's documentation of his world in Texas.

Wayne would be pleased to connect with you at wayne@sgrpublishing.com. You can also visit his website www.sgrpublishing.com.

www.ingramcontent.com/pod-product-compliance
Lightning Source LLC
Chambersburg PA
CBHW060408220326
41598CB00023B/3066